Every Cat's Survival Guide to Living with a Neurotic Owner

Every Cat's Survival Guide to Living with a Neurotic Owner

Beth Adelman

Main Street
A division of Sterling Publishing Co., Inc.
New York

Published by Main Street, a division of Sterling Publishing Co., Inc.
387 Park Avenue South, New York, NY 10016

Distributed in Canada by Sterling Publishing
c/o Canadian Manda Group, 165 Dufferin Street
Toronto, Ontario, Canada M6K 3H6

Distributed in Great Britain by Chrysalis Books Group PLC
The Chrysalis Building, Bramley Road, London W10 6SP, England

Distributed in Australia by Capricorn Link (Australia) Pty. Ltd.
P.O. Box 704, Windsor, NSW 2756, Australia

ISBN 1-4027-3133-7

Text design by Leah Lococo

Illustrations by Paul Hoffman

Manufactured in the United States of America

10 9 8 7 6 5 4 3 2 1

For information about custom editions, special sales, premium and
corporate purchases, please contact Sterling Special Sales
Department at 800-805-5489 or specialsales@sterlingpub.com.

Heavenly nose kisses to Carol Lea Benjamin, my smartest advisor, biggest cheerleader, and best friend; Pam Johnson-Bennett, who knows more about cats than anyone I've ever met; Steve Dale, who always makes me feel more important than I really am; and Craig, the best of all my husbands, who gave me the space to write this book.

Contents

PART 5
It's OK to Show Affection (And Get Attached)   179

AFTERWORD

ALL ABOUT ME, "DEAR TABBY"

I love my people—*really*. They open the cat food. They scoop the litter box. They bring home the catnip. They make the fuzzy toys wiggle. They are warm when I snuggle up next to them. They love me too, and they show it as best they can. But there's a lot humans don't know about us, and their ignorance can be downright annoying.

Sometimes I just have to ask myself, "Can't we all just get along?" And of course, we can. But it's certainly not easy. People are mysterious creatures, and they do not speak our language. While we are masters at reading their moods, and even reading their minds, they seem unable to penetrate ours. Usually they try to do their best. But because we're just not on the same wavelength, what they think is "their best" is not always what we want. And, believe it or not, sometimes their best is really better for us, and we just don't realize it.

This book is intended as a guide to help all my fellow felines live better, happier lives with their people. For more than a decade, cats and kittens all over the world have been sending me questions about their people. They ask me why their people behave the way they do, what they can do to re-train their people, and why they are not always getting exactly what they want. All the cats and kittens I've helped over the years have urged me to share my special human knowledge with the larger feline world. And, because publishing a book is an extremely dignified endeavor (and I absolutely believe cats must *always* be dignified), I have finally agreed.

Let me tell you a little about myself. I was born in a community of wild cats, but my mother was killed when I was very young. I would have been a goner were it not for the kindness of a person who swooped in one day, snatched me from my cold little nest, and brought me home to her nice warm house for some good food. I have to admit, I absolutely did not trust her at first. In my feline group, the talk was that humans were bad news, and the first lesson my mom taught me was to stay away from them. But my person convinced me that living with humans has many advantages for cats—not the least of which is that you can stop eating garbage (which is *very* undignified).

I pride myself in saying I understand these strange creatures. I know what motivates them, I know how to communicate with them, and, more important, I know how to train them. My person knows how to roll over in bed and lift the covers so I can slink under them, even when she is asleep; she responds to a simple paw signal that I taught her in just a few weeks. I'll share my training secrets with you in these pages, so you can also direct your humans to meet your needs quickly and efficiently.

How did I learn so much about humans? By watching them. I sit and stare at them when they're eating dinner. I stand over them when they are sleeping. I sit on the windowsill and quietly observe them when they are mating. I follow them into the bathroom to learn their most private habits. I hide under the dinner table with my ears wide open when they are arguing. I listen in when they think I'm sleeping. And, because they believe I don't understand, they tell me everything they are thinking. But, like most cats, I understand their language very well.

My years of close observation have taught me that humans, as irrational as they may seem, always have a reason for their behavior. If we cats can just think like a person, we can gently mold them into the companions we want them to be. They love us, and they *want* to please us. We just need to show them how.

You've Got to Have Class

DIET AND GROOMING

Most cats I know spend about a third of their waking hours grooming—which is one reason we are all so gorgeous. Compare this with our people, who jump in and out of the shower in five minutes. (I suspect this does not leave them enough time to wash carefully between every toe, the way we do.) We take hours to meticulously keep ourselves clean, making sure every single hair is washed and in place. We are exquisitely designed for this, too: We can wash our own backs, and our tongues have little barbs that help us pull out the dead hair and rearrange our coiffure.

One of our little beauty secrets is a good diet. Simply put, the best food gives us the best fur. It's expensive, but does anyone doubt that we're worth it?

My Human Is Starving Me!

Dear Tabby,

Help! I am stuck with a human who has suddenly become stingy. Babs used to make sure my food dish was full all the time, but lately she's been measuring out two meals a day and picking up my dish after half an hour! What's with this sudden obsession with my figure? I'm a longhair, and we are supposed to be pleasingly plump.

What's even more annoying is that Babs's food dish, the one where she keeps the cheese puffs, is always full. But she won't even share. Every time I manage to drag a cheese puff out of her bowl, Babs puts them someplace I can't reach. She acts as if I were doing something wrong! *Of course* I'm going to eat the cheese puffs. They're irresistibly yummy-- and Babs eats them all the time. Why won't she share her food with me? And why can't I eat whatever I want?

Sincerely famished,

Priscilla

DEAR PRISCILLA,

Sorry dear, but I've got good news and bad news. The good news is that Babs loves you a lot. The bad news is that she is showing her love by helping you lose a little weight. Being chubby is just not good for us.

How thin should you be? Well, sweetie, we pussycats should never look like starving strays (the way those skinny human models do). If you look in the mirror and you can see your ribs, plunge into that bowl of cheese puffs and put on some meat! But while ribs should not be seen, they should be felt. I suspect that when Babs takes her hand out of her food bowl and runs it down your side, she can't feel your ribs. And Pris, that's a bad sign.

Being overweight puts too much stress on our joints, heart, and lungs, and makes us much more likely to get diabetes, arthritis, liver diseases, and lots of other conditions you really don't want. And sweetie, as we get older, we're going to have a hard time keeping up our good grooming if we get too tubby. I know that's the sort of thing you longhaired girls care a lot about.

Babs is doing you a favor by measuring out your meals. Let's face it, we cats are not so great in the self-control department. Sometimes we eat when we're not hungry, just because the food is there. Maybe your human, Babs, does the same thing, and she probably wishes she had someone to measure out how much she eats. But Pris, that is not your job. Don't try to keep Babs on a diet by eating all her cheese puffs! She's got the thumbs that enable her to open the refrigerator, and you'll never be able to control what she eats. Just worry about yourself, OK?

I hope we're clear now that Babs is just trying to look out for you. So what should you do? Well, first of all, since you know your food dish is getting filled only twice a day, for heaven's sake eat what's in it. Hurry up, girl! I think you'll find that when you eat all your meals, you're not as hungry as you thought. You've probably been eating out of habit, or boredom, or because something (maybe those cheese puffs) just smells good. Everyone know that we cats can't resist yummy smells, and sometimes they make us think we're hungry when we're not.

Make sure Babs feeds you at about the same times every day. This way, you can look forward to your meals. If supper should be served at 8:00 and she still hasn't gotten around to it by 8:02, *remind her.* Try meowing loudly, walking across her face, and running back and forth between the couch and the kitchen.

If you're feeling bored or hungry between meals, find a distraction. Look out the window at the passing cars, watch the birds in a nearby tree, or toss around one of your toys. If Babs is at home, try to get her to play with you.

The exercise will be good for both of you. Bring her one of your feather toys. (You *do* have feather toys, don't you, Pris? I've never met a longhair who didn't.) Or meow at the closet where she keeps the fishing pole toys. If all else fails, start chasing Babs around the house. You'll get some good exercise, and you'll both get a good laugh.

Now, about those cheese puffs . . . A little snack now and then won't hurt you, but my diet consultant says the extras shouldn't make up more than 8 to 10 percent of your total diet. And I know you'll hate to hear this, but Babs should feed you a little less at mealtimes if she's planning to give you unscheduled treats. As for the unguarded cheese puff bowl, Pris, you can't be blamed. Nature has programmed us cats to eat whenever we can—even if we know exactly where and when our next meal is coming. You can't be expected to pass up an irresistible treat, so Babs needs to help you out by not leaving the goodies where you can get them.

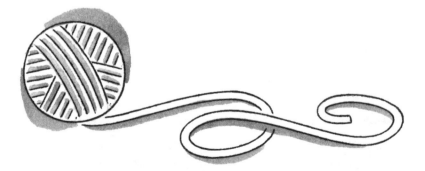

Too Fat to Groom

Dear Tabby,

This is the most embarrassing letter I've ever had to write. I've got, well, a grooming problem. I've gained a bit of weight in the past few years, and now I find I can't reach my lower back (you know, that wide area just above the tail where I love to be scratched) and also my . . . um . . . unmentionables under the tail. I've always kept myself nice and neat, but now I'm getting little mats in my fur back there. Plus, I can't always clean up the way I'd like to after a trip to the litter box. I tell you, sometimes I feel so unkempt I just want to scream! I don't feel good about myself anymore. Help!

Your trusting reader,
Bob Katz

DEAR BOB,

We cats certainly do like to keep ourselves neat—which is why we are all so gorgeous. And Bobby dear, I know it must be distressing for you to feel less than your best. But honey, let me be blunt here: You're too fat! Please read the previous letter from the lovely Miss Priscilla, because I am not going to repeat those warnings about health problems that come from being pudgy. Let's concentrate on your grooming problems first. And then, my dear Mr. Katz, we'll talk about a weight-loss diet. I can hear you howling now, but it's for your own good.

Let's talk a minute about mats. As you've probably noticed, they build up when our lovely hairs come loose but are not groomed out. All those loose hairs just build up and get tangled together, until they form a lump of hair that is most unattractive. The longer you leave them alone, the bigger they get, until they work their way down to the skin and start pulling on it—ouch, ouch! That can hurt a lot. They have to be cut out then, too, which means big patches with no fur at all. If you think you feel self-conscious now, Bob, imagine how you'll feel when you look like one of those hairless dogs. So deal with those mats before they get any bigger!

Your people need to get involved here with the grooming. They can gently comb out the little mats using a comb with metal teeth or a slicker brush. But make sure they do it very gently; if they tug and pull at your skin, give them a hiss as a warning and a swat if they still keep at it. (Keep the scratching in reserve for when they *really* don't get the message.) Your people should brush you every single day, Bob, until you slim down some.

As for that "under the tail" thing, I hate to tell you this, Bob, but your people will have to help you out there, too. I know there's nothing we hate more than having our "unmentionables" touched, but you've gotta keep it clean. What else can I say? So if anything gets stuck back there, they need to moisten a piece of paper towel with warm water and gently wipe it clean. You can whine a bit when they do this, just to let them know you're not having fun. They should also gently lift your tail and trim away the extra hair with blunt scissors. And Bobby, try not to turn this into a wrestling match, because the excess hair is *all* you want them to trim away. Need I say more?

OK, let's talk diet, because this problem is not going to go away on its own. We cats lose weight the same way people do, dearie: less food and more exercise. But we need to lose it slowly, because cats who do the starvation skinny diet can get really sick. (Not to get too technical, but when a cat misses out on too many calories, fat gets deposited in the liver, which causes liver failure. Scary!) Reducing the amount of food you eat by a quarter or less won't do you

any harm, and will do you a world of good, sweetie. No need for those yucky low-fat diets, just less food. Like Priscilla, you're going to have to eat it in measured amounts, but smaller meals throughout the day should help you feel full, fine, and, eventually, fit. And Bobby, listen up here: No between-meal snacks! Don't even start the begging routine, because you know your humans can't resist.

You need to get around more, too, Bob. I know there's a gorgeous guy inside that tubby exterior, just waiting to come out. So start chasing those flies instead of just looking at them. Get up on your people's dresser and knock off their loose change, one coin at a time. Hop up on the treadmill when a human gets on it. Leap from the bed to the windowsill to the floor to the bed again for no reason at all. It's a great workout for you, and it will drive your people crazy.

And finally, Tabby recommends that all cats pay a visit to their vet before they start a weight-loss program. Why? *Because I say so!*

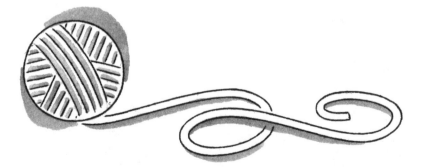

Enough with the Grain! I'm a Carnivore!

Dear Tabby,

I like cat food as much as the next puss, but no matter how much I eat, I just don't feel right. My coat is kind of dry and dull, and this really upsets me because I have beautiful black fur that just doesn't shine the way I know it should. I don't have as much energy as I used to, either. And when I go to the litter box . . . well . . . a lot of what I just ate ends up in there. One night when my people were sleeping, I looked at the cat food label and saw it has more grain in it than meat! When is the last time you saw a nature film with leopards grazing on the wild grasses of the savanna? I'm a meat eater, Tabby. Why are they feeding me grain?

Your carnivorous pal,

Spike

DEAR SPIKE,

We're all little tigers when it comes to food, aren't we? In the wild we cats catch and eat mice, rats, birds, and other small animals. We do not sit around making toast or baking cookies. In fact, for us the mouse is the perfect food, and we eat them bones, fur, innards, and all (I'm just quivering all over thinking about this!).

Mother Nature never intended cats to eat grain. Our humans can get energy and all their vitamins and minerals from plants, but we cats have the bodies—and the guts—of supreme hunters. (Hear me roar!) We are designed to use protein for energy, not the carbohydrates in grain.

I'm going to get technical here for a moment, Spike my friend, because I want you to really understand what's going on in your beautiful feline body. We cats have evolved so that our liver makes glucose (the major energy source for every mammal) mainly out of the amino acids in protein. I know that's a mouthful, but what it really means is that we simply can't adapt to a low-protein diet. It's our way or no way (as it is with so many things feline). If our people eat a diet that's low in protein, their bodies simply stop using protein. But we cats can't do that. And if there's not enough protein in our diet, we will eventually begin to metabolize our own bodies. This really is as bad as it sounds!

Of course, there is protein in some plants (think about tofu—although I try very hard not to), but not enough for us. And the proteins are incomplete (it would take me three pages to explain what that means, but trust me, it's not good for cats). There are other nutrients we kitties simply must have that just can't be found in plants, either.

If we don't get all the meat we need, we certainly do have less energy, which is what you've been experiencing, Spike. And our beautiful coats are the next thing to go; whatever protein and nutrients we are getting are being waylaid to more vital things like the heart and brain (just try living without those!), so our coats end up being dry, hard, and dull. We may even get a little dandruff. (You didn't mention that, Spike, and I don't want to embarrass you, but if you're seeing a few flakes in that gorgeous black coat, it's probably the food.)

The cat food companies are all trying to package that perfect mouse—in a way that won't make our people squeal and scream. But some of them do it better than others. In some canned foods they add things like rice, which we really don't need. And all the dry foods use some kind of grain to make those crunchy little bits stick together. A little grain won't hurt us, and I like the crunchies, but a food that's more grain than meat is going to leave us looking and

feeling less than our best. Plus, there is that unpleasant litter box effect you mentioned: If we can't really digest most of what's in the food, we simply pass it along. So our people end up scooping that food into our dish, then scooping it out of the litter box a few hours later.

I'm sure your people mean well, but they haven't been choosing the best food for you. You need to help them learn how to read the labels on cat food. The ingredients are always listed in descending order, by weight. So the number one thing to look for is a cat food that lists some kind of meat as the very first ingredient. But appearances can be deceiving, and here's where a tomcat (and his people) must be very clever. Suppose you see chicken liver listed as the first ingredient. You might think the food has more chicken liver in it than anything else. But not so! It may be followed by wheat flour, cornmeal, and corn gluten meal—and when you add up all that grain stuff, it could weigh more than the meat!

So what's a hungry boy to do? Well, look for a food that has meat as the first ingredient, and at least two meat (or fish) products among the first four ingredients. Use this information along with the Guaranteed Analysis, which is that little box that says how much protein, how much fat, and so on is in the food. Dry foods should have *at least* 30 percent protein, and wet foods should have *at least* 10 percent. Put those two things together, Spike my boy, and you will have a food that will make your coat shiny and give you the spunk of a kitten.

Now, I'll be honest here and say that those meaty cat foods cost more money. But sweetie, we're worth it. As far as I'm concerned, that's the end of that discussion. However, if you live with people who like math, explain this to them: Because the really good foods have more of what we need, we eat much less. So a big bag lasts a lot longer, and it's really not much more expensive. As I've already explained, with the cheaper foods, about half ends up in the litter box. So where's the savings? Talk about flushing your money down the toilet!

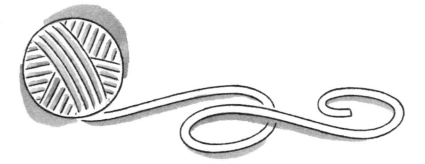

Canned Food or Dry?

Dear Tabby,

I'm confused about what kind of cat food is best for me--canned or dry. I like canned food because it's more like meat (except I don't get to tear the head off). And I really like the smell. I've heard that canned food is better for me, too, because it has more protein per bite, and because the moisture helps keep my kidneys healthy. The good canned foods go through less manufacturing and processing, too.

But I also like the dry food. It's crunchy and tasty, and chewing on it helps keep my teeth clean. And if my person leaves my food out for a few hours (which I wish he'd do more often, by the way), it doesn't end up with that nasty smell that canned food gets when it sits around.

To make things more confusing, my first veterinarian told my person to feed me only dry food. But when we moved and I got a new vet, she told my person to feed me only canned food.

So give me the lowdown, Tabby. Canned or dry?

Yours truly (confused),

Pumpkin

DEAR PUMPKIN,

When the experts don't agree, there's only one thing for a confused cat to do: Whatever he wants! My advice is to enjoy both. When I eat a mouse, I like chewing on the meaty bits, and I also like crunching on the bones.

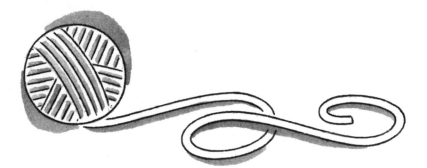

Can't I Eat What You're Eating?

Dear Tabby,

Every day I see my person, Todd, go into the kitchen, sometimes for hours, and prepare himself beautiful, fresh meals that he never shares with me. Everything I eat comes out of a can or a box, and while the cat food tastes good and I feel healthy, I still wish I could eat something that hasn't been processed or packaged.

I have asked Todd for his food several times. Sometimes I sit at one of the empty dining room chairs and put my paws on the table, the way he does, so he'll get the idea. Sometimes I just meow at him in the kitchen. Sometimes I even try to sneak a bit of meat from the kitchen counters. But he just doesn't seem to get it. Now I'm longing for a personal chef.

I don't think any of my ancestors ever ran around on the African plains with can openers in their paws. Can't I eat people food?

Sincerely tired of the cans,
Carol

DEAR CAROL,

I know some cats who adore their cat food and never crave anything else. But some cats just want to eat real meat. Human foods are excellent sources of nutrients—after all, humans do just fine on them. But we cats need the right combination of meat and other ingredients; simply tucking into a bowl of meat doesn't provide us with balanced nutrition, sweetie. Meat has plenty of protein, but it lacks many other nutrients we need, such as calcium and vitamins.

Does that mean you can't eat what your person eats? Absolutely not. If you've got a craving for people food, honey, that's fine. A little meat or fish now and then as a treat will do you some good. Fresh foods have natural enzymes that processed foods don't have. Just remember: We're talking about real meat and fish, not the gristly, greasy leftovers that Todd would normally toss in the trash. If it's good enough for him, it's good enough for you. But if he won't eat it, you shouldn't either.

What else can you eat besides meat? Dairy products are a favorite of mine. (I just love those smelly French cheeses!) But be aware that some cats simply can't digest dairy and end up with diarrhea. If you're one of those kinds of kitties, lay off the dairy entirely. Forget about all those cute Victorian Valentine's Day cards of kittens lapping up spilled milk; cats do not need to drink milk at all. If dairy doesn't upset your tummy, though, cheese, cottage cheese, yogurt, and sour cream seem to be better choices than milk for most cats.

Some cats I know like an occasional nibble of a cracker, some whole-grain breakfast cereal, or a piece of bread. We don't really get any nutrition from these kinds of things, so eat them *very* sparingly. And I've heard of cats who like to eat a green bean or a little piece of lettuce now and then. Weird, I know, but your ancestors on the African plains did occasionally seek out some fresh salad, Carol, so a bit of chopped-up greens, if you like them, are fine. Stay away from sugar at all costs (we cats simply can't digest those kinds of carbs), and remember that chocolate is toxic to all kitties.

Let Todd know you want some of that yummy food he's preparing by following him into the kitchen. Then sit up nicely and just stare at him. No jumping up on the counters or howling, because then it seems like you're being naughty, and he's less inclined to give in. Just be a perfect puss and stare deeply. Make your face say, "I love you so much. Why don't you give me what I want?" You can try adding one sweet, gentle meow, just for punctuation. This has always

worked for me. And please, Carol honey, promise me you will *never* beg for food. It's not dignified—and I believe cats must be dignified at all times. In fact, occasionally when Todd offers you something you've simply adored in the past, just sniff at it and walk away. It gives him an incentive to try extra hard to please you.

If you want to start eating some people food, you need to be sure it doesn't make up more than 15 percent of your total diet, and that the rest of what you eat is a top-quality complete and balanced cat food. This way, you'll be enjoying the fresh food and still getting what you need. That's the best of everything—which is exactly what all cats deserve!

Can you eat an entirely homemade diet? If Todd is willing to work hard for you (and why not?), the answer is yes. You just need to keep in mind that cats cannot live by meat alone. Remember, Carol, in the wild we eat our prey whole—including the fur, skin, bones, guts (rodent spleen is a feline delicacy in many parts of the world), and even the contents of the stomach. Any homemade diet will have to include supplements that provide the same nutrients as those nonmeat mouse parts. And it will have to be carefully balanced, with all the right nutrients in just the right amounts. It requires a lot of research to get a homemade diet just right, but it can be done. Tabby recommends working with a veterinary nutritionist. This is serious stuff!

My Water Dish Is a Stagnant Pond

Dear Tabby,

My water dish looks like a stagnant pond. There's hair and dust floating in it, but that's just the top layer. When I brush all that away, there are ancient bits of waterlogged cat food lying on the bottom, and a bug that went for a swim about two weeks ago and drowned. Every time I go near that dish, I keep expecting something creepy to jump out of it and bite me on the nose. I'm so thirsty, but I just can't drink that water.

I've taken to jumping up on the side of the sink when my people run the water, so I can get a clean drink from the faucet. I drink from their water glasses when they put them down (how come their water is always cleaner than mine?), and, although I hate to admit it, I sometimes even drink out of the toilet bowl. What does a thirsty cat have to do to get a decent drink?

Your parched pal,
Scotty

DEAR SCOTTY,

You've made a good start by refusing to drink out of your water dish, but your people seem to need a little more help to get the message. Wait until they can see you, and then try splashing the water around with your paws; make as big a mess as you can, and then walk away.

You can also try the "silent vigil" approach. Sit down in front of your water dish and look at it mournfully. When your people pass by, look up at them with a mixture of discontent and disgust. Make your face say, "You expect me to drink this? I am saddened and disappointed."

If all else fails, simply tip the dish over. If nothing else, this will force your people to refill it with clean water.

Listen up, cats and kittens, because this is vital. All cats must have clean water all the time. We don't drink much (after all, we were descended from wild cats who lived in a dry climate and knew how to be very frugal with their water supply), but what we do drink has got to be pristine. We absolutely must have our water dish refilled *several* times a day, and scrubbed clean once a day. You need to explain it to your people this way, Scotty: When they want a glass of water, they expect fresh water and a clean glass. You should not have to expect any less.

Your problem with the waterlogged food illustrates a pet peeve of mine (and peeves are the only pets I keep!): those side-by-side food and water dishes. Just say no and no. It's too easy for your food to get into your water; plus those bowls are usually plastic, and plastic eventually gets to be a welcoming home to millions of tiny bacteria that don't wash away. And those bacteria very well *could* jump out and bite you on the nose, sweetie. You need separate food and water dishes, made of ceramic or stainless steel.

Finally, Scotty dear, let me fill you in on two very important points. First, every time you go over to look at your water, you drop your hair into it. You can't help it. So learn to tolerate a teeny bit of hair—maybe just one or two—on the surface. And second, never—and I do mean *never*—drink from the toilet bowl. Humans use really nasty chemicals to clean their watery litter box, but the main reason is that it's just not dignified.

What's All the Fuss About Nail Clipping?!

Dear Tabby,

I really hate it when my people clip my nails. I just don't like being held still and having my paws touched that way, and the clipper makes those sharp little sounds that are kind of scary. I've tried making a big fuss about it, moaning and howling and putting up a struggle, and I have scratched my people a few times in the process--not on purpose, but just because the whole thing makes me so upset. But they still insist on pulling out the clippers. I'm the claw man. How do I make them stop?

Your sincere swordsman,
Nero

DEAR NERO,

How do you make them stop? The short answer is that you don't. Nero, my dear, having your nails clipped is a very good thing. We kitties are justifiably proud of the fact that we can grow nails as beautiful and sharp as a samurai's sword. But unless they're trimmed, our nails just keep getting longer and sharper. And that can lead to some unintentional but nasty scratches—not just on your people, but on you. When you scratch that sweet spot right in front of your ear, for instance, if your nails are too long you can really hurt yourself. Some cats' nails grow so long that they actually curl back into the pads. I can't even imagine how painful that is! And if the nails on your dewclaws (those little extra claws some of us have a little farther up our front legs) get too long, they can snag in something and actually tear. Ouch! I know you don't want that, Nero.

Your people probably also realize that when they play with you, if those little razor-sharp tips aren't snipped off, you'd be scratching them all the time by accident. Plus, if you get a little excited and scratch a piece of furniture, those extrasharp claws can do a lot of damage very quickly. You live with these people, Nero, and they put out the cat food; you don't want to go shredding them and their stuff.

A young friend of mine, Mei Mei, refused to have her claws clipped. One day she decided to explore the possibilities presented by a large bug that was settled outside a window screen in her house. She got those long claws caught in the screen and had to yowl for her people to come untangle her. Now, we must ask ourselves: Is this dignified? Definitely not!

Nero, you're going to have to take a chill pill when it comes to trimming. They are giving you a manicure, and you should accept this as the pampering that is every cat's birthright. And honey, you will still be armed and dangerous with clipped claws. Tough guys also get manicures.

Sometimes it helps to start from scratch and get rid of all those nasty feelings you've built up about this. (In fact, if your people had started trimming your nails sooner, when you were still a young kit, you probably wouldn't have this negative reaction now!) Close your eyes and reach back to your inner kitten. Let your people start by just lightly touching your paws, one at a time, and very, very gently squeezing the pads to expose the nails. Next, let's try it one paw at a time: just a quickie trim of the four tootsies on a single paw, then a delicious snack to make you feel this was all a good thing. In four days, all four paws will be a little less lethal.

Some cats just don't like the way they are held for trimming. You didn't mention how your people hold you, Nero, but if they turn you on your back, I completely understand. We cats feel really vulnerable in that position, no

matter how much we love our people. Calm cats like being held in a nice, wide lap or against their person's body. For those who fuss a bit more, like you, try lying on your side with one person just holding you gently at the shoulders and hips and one person clipping away. If you and your person live alone, of course, this isn't possible. (Unlike us, people use only two of their arms for doing things.) In that case, your person can put a little treat on the floor and simply kneel over you to reach your paws.

You didn't say what color your nails are, dear, but that may explain some of your discomfort. The next time you're sitting in the windowsill, unsheathe those awesome claws and look at them in the sunlight. See how they form a perfect curl and taper to an elegant, deadly point. Meeeowowow! If they are white, you'll see a beautiful pink line running up from the bottom. That's where the nerves and blood vessels are, so it's important not to cut that part. If your nails are dark, make sure your people only cut off the tips—just to be on the safe side.

Many cats have written to me over the years to inquire how often they need a manicure. Tabby says, when you can hear your nails clicking on the floor, it's time for a trim.

Keep Your Brush to Yourself

Dear Tabby,

I'm just not crazy about being brushed. The problem is, at least twice a week my person tries to pick me up, hold me in her lap, and go over me with a huge brush. I hate this, and I've let her know by swatting her on the hand, struggling, and jumping out of her lap as soon as I can get away. But sometimes she holds me there and insists on brushing me.

My person is a female longhair, and she brushes herself several times a day. It's a good thing, too, because when she wakes up in the morning, her hair looks like a pile of sleeping kittens. But I'm a shorthaired cat; I groom myself every day, and I just don't see why extra brushing is necessary. What do you think?

Your beauty buff,
Stella

DEAR STELLA,

Are you mad? How could you not simply adore being brushed? As far as I'm concerned, my people don't take out the grooming brush nearly as often as I'd like. A lovely brushing is like a full body massage. You should relax, purr, and feel the good vibrations.

I suspect your real problem, Stella, is not with the brushing, but with the fact that you are being swept off your feet. Silly young humans may love that sort of thing, but we cats prefer to be firmly on our four paws at all times. It's a question of control. I know some cats who have a special table they hop onto when they are being brushed, or a grooming chair. My people treat me with the proper deference when I am being brushed, and place me on the top platform of my cat tree. I feel secure and admired, and can thoroughly relax. It is really easy to train your person to brush you in the specific spot you choose. Simply run to that spot whenever she takes out the brush, then settle there and refuse to budge.

You mentioned that your person uses a huge brush, and this may be part of your problem. Cats are small creatures, and we need small brushes. A human brush or (and I shudder to even think about this) a dog brush simply will not do. Most cats really like what the humans call a slicker brush. A slicker brush has a rectangular head with lots of long, thin, bent pins stuck in it. Humans think they look scary, but trust me, they feel sooooo good! And they're simply marvelous for pulling out all that nasty undercoat that's hard for even us shorthairs to get with our main grooming tool—our tongue. Cats with especially thin coats, like the Devon Rex, older cats, or very sensitive pussies may prefer a rubber brush with little nubbles, or a bristle brush.

Believe me, Stella, brushing is good for you, and you're going to love it. Yes, you get plenty of that dead hair out when you groom, but sweetie, you swallow it all. How much hair do you really want in your stomach? Eventually, it's got to come out. And that means hairballs (ack! ack!), or something worse: obstructions. Those are really nasty hairballs that are too big or too far down to cough up. Then we're talking about a serious trip to the veterinarian's office. I don't know about you, Stella, but the vet's is definitely not my favorite place.

An added bonus for your person is that less of your hair will be all over the house. It's nice to see the real color of the couch every once in a while, isn't it?

My advice is to start slow. Just a few strokes and then let your longhair person know you've had enough by simply walking away. Eventually, as you relax and realize how great this feels, you're going to be able to sit still for more. Try rubbing the sides of your face against the brush for an extra delight. Purrrrrrrrrr!

And finally, remember, this is a service our people provide for us. We want to encourage them in that direction, sweetie. It's best for all cats when we do.

I've Got Hairballs, and I'm Proud of It!

Dear Tabby,

I sometimes get hairballs. No big deal, right? We all swallow hair when we groom ourselves. We all sometimes have to cough it up. I particularly like to cough mine up when my people have guests over for dinner. It's the excitement and the attention I love. I start to hack quietly, then gradually bring up the volume, and then, when everyone is looking at me, the long, slithery hairball rises from my throat like a monster in a scary movie. Everybody at the table makes strange noises (I think they're admiring my work), and then my people jump up and pick it up as quick as they can. I really like it when they clean up after me, and to show my appreciation I'm always careful to get off the sofa or the rug and only toss my hairballs on the nice wood floor.

My problem is that lately I've had the sense that my people are less than pleased with my performance. There is even talk of taking me to the veterinarian. What do you think?

Your drama queen,

Pookie

DEAR POOKIE,

So, you love to cough up your hairballs in front of company. Don't we all! I simply adore the drama of it. However, if you want to avoid a trip to the vet, you'll need to keep the hairballs to a minimum—maybe one grandly dramatic dinner a month. An occasional hairball once or twice a month may be a dinner party crisis, but it is absolutely not a health crisis. However, if you're hacking more often, a checkup is not a bad idea.

The hair we swallow during grooming is supposed to come out the other end, in our litter box. And there are some things we can do to keep those little fuzzies moving in the right direction.

The first is lots of grooming service from your people. They should use a slicker brush or a fine-tooth comb to really pull out all the loose hair in your lovely coat. Less hair on your body means less hair in your tummy, dear Pookie. It's that simple.

It's easy to train your people to groom you more often. Start by encouraging them to take out the brush. Go over to the closet or drawer where they keep your grooming tools and paw at it persistently. You may also have to start off with a demanding meow (trainers call this a voice command) to get their attention. When they take out the brush and comb, give them lots of praise and encouragement so they will realize they have done the right thing (trainers call this positive reinforcement). Come running over to them and rub against their legs seductively. As they are brushing you, purr sweetly and look into their eyes. Occasionally, press the top of your head into their hands. It may take time for your people to learn the entire sequence, but, as with all training, your patience and persistence will pay off. Eventually you will be able to use the simple nonverbal command of pawing at the brush drawer, and they will know exactly what you want.

There are also some things you can eat to help push along the hair you swallow when you groom. Basically, there are slippery things and bulky things. The slippery stuff is petroleum jelly, which coats the hair and helps whisk it away to its exit. We can't digest petroleum jelly, so it makes the whole trip all the way to the end—escorting all that hair out with it. There are some companies that make petroleum jelly flavored with malt, liver, and even tuna just for us cats to enjoy, and a little lick each day should keep everything moving.

There are also hairball treats made with mineral oil. It's the same idea, except mineral oil is a bit more of a laxative, so don't eat too many of these, Pookie, or you know what will happen. Also, both mineral oil and petroleum jelly tend to gather up some important vitamins with them on
their trip through our
tummy, so you don't want

to have your hairball remedy around mealtimes. You need your vitamins, sweetie.

The bulky stuff is fiber. The idea here is that it sticks to the hair and helps move it along. Those new hairball control diets have different kinds of fiber that's added to help keep things moving along. Of course, the whole point of fiber is that we don't digest it, and adding a lot of stuff to our food that we can't digest means taking out some stuff that we can digest. It's something to consider.

So what's the bottom line here, Pookie? *Moderation.*

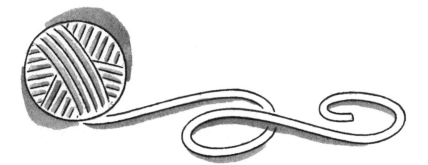

Is Neutering Bad for Me?

Dear Tabby,

My people are arguing about having me neutered. In other words, they want to snip off my little eggs. I know what it sounds like, but Pam says it's a good thing, and will help me stay happy and healthy. Pam thinks the neutering will help me calm down, too. But Steve says it will make me less of a male, and he thinks that's not fair.

The truth is, I have these urges to do crazy things all the time, like roam around the neighborhood fighting with other cats and pee on the walls of my house. I just can't control myself. I know something's up, and I figure it has to do with this neutering thing. Pam wants to have it done right away, and says I will feel better. But I'm really confused. Is neutering a bad thing?

Your raging hormone,

Zeke

DEAR ZEKE,

It sounds to me as if Steve is worried about Pam neutering him, not you.

The people we live with tend to think our world is just like theirs. And humans, the males especially, have built their whole culture around sex. They think that when we're neutered, we'll miss those long nights of love that they seem to enjoy so much.

What Steve doesn't seem to understand is that love, for us cats, is about cuddling and petting and purring. Sex is purely about instinct, and we don't get any pleasure from it. In fact, it can be downright painful.

When our hormones are raging, we feel uncomfortable, unhappy, and obsessed. After we mate, we feel less uncomfortable, unhappy, and obsessed. That's it. We don't bathe in the afterglow of romance. We don't have the urge to smoke cigarettes and tell witty stories about ourselves. We don't wonder if the cat we just mated with will call us again. In fact, we don't give it another thought.

Neutering is the right choice for every cat who is not part of a carefully planned breeding program. Sex is definitely something we do very well without.

The humans have made up all kinds of myths to convince themselves that not neutering us is OK. It sounds like your Steve person has been hearing those tall tales and thinks they're true. So, for the record, cats and kittens, neutering does not make us fat and lazy, stunt our growth, give us litter box problems, take away our natural instincts, cause us to act like silly kittens, or make us want to bite.

Meanwhile, it does protect you boys from all kinds of cancers and other diseases you can get "down there," keeps you from roaming and fighting, extends your life span, and leaves you with no reason whatsoever to mark every upright surface with your smelly scent (which should make both Pam and Steve happy).

For us girls, spaying protects us from plenty of female complaints and cancers as well—especially breast cancer. Plus, it extends our life and keeps us from going crazy twice a year. A cousin of mine wasn't spayed, and when she went into heat, all she could do was howl all night and howl all day. She felt so bad that she couldn't eat and couldn't get comfortable enough, even for an hour, to sleep. She'd just pace around the house howling and sticking her behind in the air, waiting for any old tom to come along. I can't imagine anything more undignified!

And it doesn't go away, girls. No, we just keep cycling again and again until we degrade ourselves with some nasty boy who happens to wander by.

Some humans think we need to have a litter of kittens before we are spayed. *Au contraire!* Having kittens actually increases our risk of getting breast cancer. It risks our health, ruins our beautiful coat, and does nothing for our disposition—other than to make us aggressive around humans when we have the kittens.

We also need to think about the hundreds of thousands of our fellow cats who are in jail right now with a death sentence simply because they have no place to live. This makes me cry every time I think about it. And if we're not part of the solution, we're part of the problem.

This is a simple operation for both the boys and the girls—trust me, I've had it done. Veterinarians do hundreds of them every year, and we're up and around the next day.

So Zeke and all you cats and kittens, tell your humans you want to skip the indignity, skip the little ones, skip the raging hormones, and just say yes to neutering.

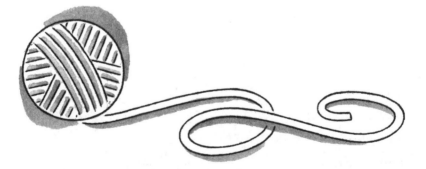

Boredom—Faking vs. the Real Thing

For us, play is always about hunting. Of course, some of us have different hunting styles or prefer different types of prey, but at heart, when we play, we're stalking our prey, planning our attack, then pouncing and going in for the kill. We *are* carnivores, after all. (I am Tabby, hear me roar!)

Play can also help us get closer to our people. We learn to watch each other's reactions and communicate better. We like to make up games, and it's not difficult to teach our people the rules—if they pay attention. Play helps us laugh together (people can be *very* amusing sometimes), and gives us a chance to show off our finely tuned feline sense of humor.

Play keeps our minds and bodies active and fit, too. Just because we spend a major part of the day sleeping in the sun doesn't mean we don't need playtime. A cat with no prey to hunt is not a happy cat.

Home Alone (Not Again!)

Dear Tabby,

I guess my problem is pretty typical of many cats: I'm home alone all day, every day. I groom a few hours each day, I sleep a lot, of course, and I try to move around the house during the day to make sure I'm always napping in the sun. I do bat my toys around a bit, but it's just not the same as when my people play with me. Basically, I don't know what to do with myself all day.

Sometimes I invent games, such as pushing everything off my person's desk or unrolling the toilet paper. Strangely, my person does not seem to find this as amusing as I do. And anyway, even that stuff is pretty unsatisfying after a while. Mostly, I'm always bored. What can I do?

Yours always (bored),

BJ

DEAR BJ,

Much as we'd like our people to be home all day, every day, to serve our needs, they must go out sometimes. They have to work to earn money for our cat food, litter, and toys, and they have to shop for our cat food, litter, and toys. These are important considerations.

Your people need to provide more and better entertainment for you in their absence. There are some home entertainment systems I highly recommend.

The first is a sturdy cat tree with several levels. The top level should be tall enough that you can lie on it and get a good view out the window. People sometimes don't understand what a lovely piece of furniture a cat tree is and how nicely it can fit into their home decor. So they try to stick it in some dark corner of the house, where it offers no entertainment whatsoever. Make sure your cat tree is by the window. Do this by refusing to go on it until your humans place it in the right spot. Cat trees are expensive, and your people will be very upset if you don't use it, so it shouldn't take long to get your point across. Sit in the windowsill, or try running from the base of the cat tree to the windowsill, but *do not* get onto the cat tree until they move it next to the window. When they do, immediately jump up on it and start rubbing your cheeks on it and purring. Make your face say, "I adore this fabulous window perch you bought me."

If there's a lot going on outside your window, relax and

enjoy the view. If not, another home entertainment system I recommend is a bird feeder. Your people can place it on a high pole near the window and fill it up, then you can sit and watch those silly birds come pecking away. If you live in an apartment building, dear, there are also bird feeders that fit right on the outside of an apartment window. I have a bird feeder outside my widow that I simply adore. Birds are pretty to watch and fun to stalk, and I don't really care that I can't catch them. (I am, after all, well fed, and what would I do with a mouth full of feathers?) Whenever I feel bored, I sit on the top level of my cat tree and watch the birds flit back and forth.

There are also videos made especially for home-alone cats. The best ones have lots of different scenes that change frequently, plenty of small movements and soft rustling and squeaking. The movement and the soft noises are what most cats seem to really like. Personally, I don't care for these videos, but many cats do. And my humans really love them. Whenever they put one on, they watch all the little squirrels and bees and fish bustling about, while I sit with my back to the TV and clean between my toes.

Certainly, if you like these videos, your person should buy you a nice selection. I heard some human say once that television rots your brain, but if that were true, I think all the humans would be dead by now. So that must be a myth. Anyway, most of these cat videos are *educational* shows; they teach you about wildlife and how to be a better hunter.

You might consider getting yourself some pets to amuse you. I do not recommend caged birds or small critters, because the temptation to eat them is just too great. You are, after all, a cat, BJ, and you cannot be expected to ignore your feline instincts in these situations.

Fish can be nice pets for a cat. They come in bright colors and move around a lot, which can be very entertaining. Plus, they do not try to get in bed with your person, take your place on the couch, or demand attention that would best be paid to you. No, fish are strictly cat pets. But I will offer a few caveats: Try to refrain from eating the fish in the fish tank. They may taste good, but they have lots and lots of tiny little bones that can get caught in your throat. Plus, if you fall in the tank, it is *impossible* to remain dignified.

Finally, you might consider a pet cat of your own. This is a very individual decision. Certainly, not all cats want another feline in the house. But some really like the company. A second cat is excellent for playing games of chase, hide, stalk, and pounce. Another cat will groom the insides of your ears (which are *so* difficult to reach) and will snuggle up next to you when your people aren't home and the house is chilly. On the other hand, another cat will take up some of your person's attention. And there is the territory issue—some cats simply do not want another puss on their turf. As I said, it is a very personal decision.

If you are considering a pet cat for yourself, BJ, get a kitten of the opposite sex. It's easier to show a little one who's boss in the house. And make sure the introductions are slow and friendly. (I'll explain more about that in Parts Four and Five, so keep reading.) You may find you really like having someone in the house who speaks your language.

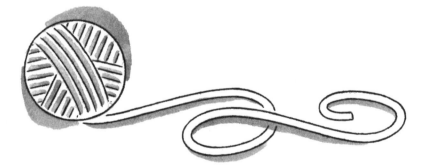

I Don't Like to
Play with Myself

Dear Tabby,

   My person buys me a lot of toys, but
they're all set up so I have to play with them
by myself. There are those little stuffed
things that hang from the doorknob, and I do
like to swat at them occasionally, but they
get boring pretty quickly. She also bought me
a scratching post with a thing at the top that
flies around in a circle. The little feather
on the end looks a bit like a bird, which is
really cool. But the problem is that the bird
always flies in the same circle, and pretty
soon it's no challenge to catch it. I'm a
hunter, Tabby, and when the hunt is too easy,
why bother?

   Lately she's been buying these really weird
toys that start to move and make noise when I
get near them. Mostly, they're too big to bat
around or swat or pick up and shake. Plus,
they're made of hard plastic, which I just
can't sink my teeth into. Tabby, I have never
seen a mouse made of plastic! And anyway,
these kinds of toys are too loud and too

strange for me. I'll be taking a nice nap, and a big truck will drive by outside, and suddenly that toy is making a racket and spinning around--it drives me crazy! Sometimes I'm afraid to walk into a room with those toys.

I know my person spends a lot of money on these toys, but they just don't interest me. All I really want is for her to play with me.

Yours, bored and ignored,

Misty

DEAR MISTY,

Humans seem to enjoy playing with themselves, but I can't say it's ever been a favorite of the felines I know. You've got two problems here: The first is that your person doesn't spend enough time playing with you. The second is that play-by-yourself toys are too predictable. So here's my advice: When you solve the first problem, you'll solve the second one, too.

Let's remember, first of all, that play is like hunting. Prey is clever—not as clever as a cat, but clever enough to make the hunt interesting. Mice, spiders, and the other creatures we love to chase are unpredictable. They run at different speeds. They change their direction. They scurry under the couch or behind the curtains. They play dead and then suddenly jump up and make a break for it.

All those wind-up, hang-on-the-door, and motion-detector toys don't do any of these things. Most follow a simple pattern when they move. But we cats are extremely intelligent hunters (of course!), and we can figure out the patterns of their movements in about thirty seconds. And then, as you said sweetie, it's just no challenge to hunt them.

Even the toys that are a little bit unpredictable are not at all like prey, because they're so big and hard (have you ever seen a lion pounce on a plastic garbage can?), and so loud (mice *do not* roar). We like things that are small and furry and make just the slightest rustle and squeak.

Humans think we hear the way they do, little Misty, but our superior cone-shaped ears pick up sounds that are much softer and much higher than their flat little ears can hear. Our people will never hear the exquisite sound of a tiny mouse trembling in the grass. And meanwhile, we think having those noisy toys in the house is like living next to an airport.

Misty, honey, you need to show your human which toys you really love, and then train her to spend more time playing with you. To begin with, never, ever touch those expensive toys—not even a little tap with your paw. Don't even sniff at them. In fact, if they're lying in the middle of the floor, take the long way around the room to avoid them. That should get the message across.

If you have any smaller, more interesting toys that you do like, play with them exclusively. Bat them around when your person is watching. If you don't have any toys you really love, find something around the house that you do love. A rolled-up sock can be fun, a piece of household fluff (every good household has fluff!), a little tidbit dragged from the trash can, a bit of paper, a leaf from one of the houseplants—all of these can make excellent toys.

Most cats (including me) really love feathers on sticks and little toys dangling from the ends of strings. Your person has to make these move, of course, and that's why

they're so much fun. She can drag them across the floor, behind the sofa, around the chair leg, and behind the curtains.
She can make them wiggle a lot or wiggle just a little. Let me
tell you, Misty dear, a good game of tickle feather will keep
me occupied for half an hour or more, and I simply love it!

Now let's talk about teaching your person to play with
you more often. The key here is positive reinforcement (we
talked about this in Part One), so that your person gets
something she likes as a reward for doing what you want.
(You may also have to use negative reinforcement, when you
annoy your person incessantly until she does what you want.)

Wait until your person is ready and able to play. Excellent choices are when she's watching the television or reading
the newspaper. When she's in the shower is not a good
choice. Pick up the toy you want to play with and throw it in
the air. Toss it in your person's lap. Bat it around a little bit.
Show her what you want her to do. Make your body language say, "I promise this will be fun!" Then stop and just
stare at her with the toy at your feet. If you want to play with
a dangling toy, drag it over to her. Look up at her with great
longing. Make your face say, "If you play with me, I'll be the
happiest cat in the world."

Now here comes the key part. When she picks up the
toy and starts playing, make sure to reward her. Leap about.
Pounce wildly. Be charming. Make her laugh. Dash from one
end of the room to the other. Lie on your back and swat at

the toy. You can even be a little silly (not *too* silly, of course—but a little silly is still dignified). Remember, Misty, you want this to be a positive experience for your person.

If she doesn't catch on and pick up the toy, you will have to resort to negative reinforcement. Meowing often works. Meow pitifully at first, because a play for sympathy can be very effective. But then start howling, louder and louder, and don't stop until your person does what you want. Other kinds of negative reinforcement include dropping the toy on her face or in her food dish and leaving it under the covers in the bed where she will roll onto it in the middle of the night. Keep this up until she gets the idea.

When you train your person to play with you on command, you both will enjoy a closer, happier relationship. And the valuable lesson your person will be learning is that *she* is your favorite toy.

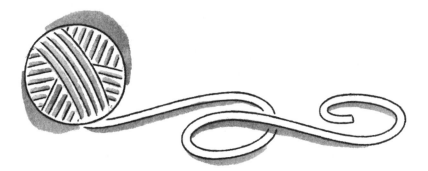

Is Outside Better Than Inside?

Dear Tabby,

Recently my person and I moved to a new house in the suburbs (we used to live in the city), and now Marisa thinks I should go outside. She keeps opening the door and encouraging me to go out. I'm not sure why she wants me to do this, because I never used to go outside before when we lived in the city, and I don't think I want to go outside now. After all, I'm not a wild animal like a squirrel or a pigeon. I'm a cat, and cats live in the house.

Still, I have to admit, some pretty interesting smells waft in when Marisa opens that door. It might be fun to sniff them out. And I have seen some other cats from our neighborhood roaming around. What do you think?

Definitely a house cat,
Darla

DEAR DARLA,

Trust me, honey, outside is vastly overrated. I was born outside, and I couldn't wait to get in. Is there some reason we have bothered to domesticate ourselves, if not to enjoy the good life away from danger, out of the rain, and on the comfy chair?

Face it, sweetie, you spend three-quarters of your life sleeping, anyway, and several hours a day grooming. Is there a better place to sleep than on the couch, in the sun? And why groom at all if you're sitting in a pile of dead leaves to do it? Do you really want to come home with bits of dead plants stuck to your backside? How dignified is that?

Marisa has probably seen some TV commercial with an adorable kitten chasing butterflies through an open field and thinks outside will be like that for you. But do you know what's outside? Big, tough cats who live on the street, even bigger tough dogs, cars, trucks, broken glass, puddles of antifreeze, automatic garage door openers, snail poison and pesticides and insecticides, toxic fertilizers, tempting (but rotten) garbage, sudden storms, fleas, ticks, diseases, teenagers with a bad attitude, foxes and coyotes and badgers and giant, nasty city rats.

You know what happens to cats who go outside? They get killed! This is not my opinion, Darla, this is a fact. The average life span of a cat who stays at home is twelve to sixteen years, but the average life span of a cat who goes outside is three to five years. Do these sound like good odds?

What gets me is that humans would never dream of

letting their dogs, their birds, their pet rabbits, their gerbils, or their kids just roam around outside with no one to watch over them, but they expect us to go out with no protection at all, as if we were wild animals—which we most definitely are *not*.

There's something else to think about, as well: The neighbors might not enjoy your using their garden as a litter box and chasing away the chipmunks. In fact, the neighbors may be completely uncivilized and not even like cats.

If you simply must get out of the house, I insist your person come with you. I'm talking about a backyard here, with a tall fence around it that goes all the way down into the ground and all the way up higher than you can jump. This is not to fence you in, Darla, but to keep you safe. You don't want the neighborhood stray cats, dogs, raccoons, and other nasty creatures wandering into your yard. And you don't want to get out by accident (perhaps when you're chasing a squirrel and forget where you are in the excitement), then end up someplace scary and unfamiliar. And you should *never* be outside alone. Like all cherished family members, you need to be watched and protected when you're out in the big bad world.

For you cats and kittens who live in apartment buildings (as I do), try the hallway. I happen to like running up and down the stairs. It's a little change of scenery, and there are interesting smells in the hallway. Plus, it's a good workout. Humans spend hundreds of dollars on machines that force them to run up the stairs for hours; we can do it for free.

Let's Party All Night

Dear Tabby,

I'm a typical cat. I like to sleep all day and party all night. The problem is that my people seem to live their lives backwards. They are awake and running around all day and like to sleep all night.

They play with me when they come home from work, but that's not when I'm at my best. I've been sleeping all day, and I get more and more revved up as the night goes on.

I've tried to teach them how to play at night. I drag my toys into their bed. I run across their faces in the middle of the night. I sit in the windowsill and sing to them. But they're just not getting it. They yell at me, and sometimes they even close me out of their bedroom. I've tried scratching and howling at the bedroom door, but they do not come out to play. Can you explain how to train them to play with me at night?

Your party animal,
Houdini

DEAR HOUDINI,

Timing is everything, my little party animal. Almost any time is a good time to play, but the best playtime for us is when we're wide-awake and feeling frisky.

Our ancestors hunted at night and slept most of the day (I still cannot understand why humans prefer to sleep in the dark, when sleeping in the sun is such a supreme pleasure!), then woke up and went out on the prowl. Maybe they chased a few different things before they finally managed to catch their dinner. We cats are designed for quick bursts of energy, so they rested between each chase. After eating, they groomed themselves clean (of course!) and then settled in for a quick nap.

Dearie, your natural rhythms are still like that. The problem is that your people live by a very different clock. They come home from work and play with you—that's like the first stalk-and-hunt session for you. Then you relax while they eat dinner. Then they lie down on the couch to watch TV, and you're ready for the next chasing game. It's even worse if they feed you at the same time they eat; you have your quick after-meal nap while they're on the couch, wake up just when they're going to bed, and are ready for more chasing and stalking and pouncing.

The answer, of course, is that you need more fun and games later in the evening. And that means you should be your most charming, your most engaging, your most irresistible right when they settle down on the couch. Prance about, turn your head upside down, lie on your back, toss your toys in the air. Make your face say, "I'm so adorable, you've simply got to play with me *now*." A couple of good play sessions just before your people go to bed will help work off some of that excess energy that keeps a party puss like you so busy at night.

A late-night snack is also a good idea. If your people leave food out for you all the time, they should pick it up when they come home from work and then give you a nice dinner just before they go to bed. If you're eating measured meals, the last one should be late in the evening. Then you've had your play/hunt time, you've had your meal, and it's time for a quick bath and a long night's nap.

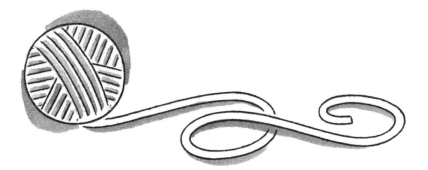

I Crave a Cave

Dear Tabby,

I live in an apartment, but sometimes I wish I didn't. You see, tents, tunnels, and caves are my thing, but my people have filled the apartment with couches, chairs, and tables. I'd love to play in a cave, where I could watch my prey slink by and then pounce out and give it good shake.

Plus, I'm a little shy sometimes, and while I love to be out in the same room as my people, I feel better if I'm in my own little protected spot. I guess tents and caves make me feel safe and excited, all at once. But, short of going camping in the woods (which doesn't seem very appealing), what can I do?

Your perplexed cave cat,

Pebbles

DEAR PEBBLES,

Many cats (myself included) just love caves, tents, and tunnels. We adore surprises, especially when we are the ones doing the surprising, and popping out from a tent or cave is an exciting surprise. This is all related to the way wild cats hunt. We have bodies that were designed to slink, hide, and pounce. We do fine in a quick chase, but we can't keep it up over long distances. So the best hunting strategy for us is to sneak up on our prey, then quickly and efficiently pounce on it and dispatch it. The best way to sneak up, of course, is to stay out of sight. So we move silently though the tall grass (and we keep low to the ground even when we're stalking something across the bare floor), and we pounce out from behind trees, bushes, and rocks. The problem is that most apartments don't have a lot of trees, bushes, and rocks.

Hunting from behind a barrier also provides protection when we're trying to kill something a little bigger than a spider or a mouse. Consider, for example, cat vs. rat. Some rats are close to us in size (some rats are even bigger than we are, but I don't even want to *think* about those!), and they can deliver a nasty bite. We go in for the kill with a bite and a shake right behind a prey animal's neck, but getting that close to a rat's face can be a dangerous proposition. So our hunting cousins corner the rat behind a barrier and then pummel it into submission with some swift paw punches before they move in for the killing bite. That barrier, the one we reach around to throw our punches, protects us if the rat decides to turn around and take a bite out of us! (That's also why we poke and prod our prey before finishing it off. Some ghoulish humans think we are torturing the animal, but we're simply protecting ourselves in a very dignified manner.)

Pebbles, my dear, do you see how tents and caves figure into all this? They're places we can hide in and pounce out from. They provide concealment and protection for us when we're playing at being the hunter. They create "bases" we can run between when we're inventing new games. They also give a shy kitty like you a safe place from which to look out on the world.

Since the average living room is just not set up like a rain forest or savanna, or even like a typical urban jungle, your people will have to be a little creative. A cardboard box set on its side makes a nice cave. It's even nicer if it's turned upside down and they cut a small opening in one side. Two or three boxes taped together with openings cut to connect them make a bigger cave or a nice tunnel, depending on how you look at it. A hard-sided cat carrier set on the floor with the door propped open also makes a very nice cave— and has the added advantage of making the carrier a more pleasant place.

As for tents, a towel is all that's required. Your peo-ple can drape it over a low

coffee table or across the seat of a dining-room chair. Or they can hang it on the back of the chair like an overcoat.

Now, Pebbles dear, you have a fine feline hunting ground. Get behind the flap of your tent and watch your people wiggle your toys just beyond your reach. There is your prey! Teach them not to keep the toy in constant motion, but rather, have it hide around furniture or sit still for a few seconds. Get down low so you're ready to pounce and follow its movement around the outside of the tent, daring you to come and attack. Wait until it seems to be slowing down a bit and then burst out—to your triumph! Or you can simply extend a paw under the tent and trap your helpless prey! Meeowrrrrrrr!

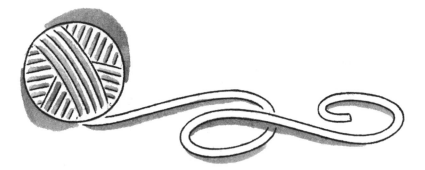

I Just Want to
Kill Something

Dear Tabby,

Sometimes I just want to kill something. I guess it's the tiger in me. I
dream of slinking through the tall grass,
stalking some unsuspecting little creature,
and then pouncing for the kill. I'd grab
my prey by the back of the neck, give a
quick shake, and then devour the little
creature at leisure. My problem is that
there's nothing around here to execute. I
live inside, and we don't have any mice.
Any ideas?

Frustrated and frazzled,

Fritz

DEAR FRITZ,

Well of course you want to kill something! Every cat gets that feeling now and then. It's not a problem—depending, of course, on what you want to kill. (Stay away from kittens, and try not to smother any houseguests your person invites over.)

Listen, my frustrated serial killer, we are hunters by nature. All the things that make us beautiful and elegant and mysterious—our full-moon eyes, our slinky spines, our graceful way of leaping, our lightning-fast reflexes—are gifts designed to make us more efficient hunters. We have all this talent, no wonder we want to use it!

Some indoor cats I know still have mouse duties to perform, but since that's not the case in your house, let me suggest some alternatives. First, dear Fritz, have you looked into the possibility of bugs? Take it from Tabby, bugs can be very satisfying prey. The tiny ones, like ants, move slowly and are not very hard to catch, but it's fascinating to watch them crawl across the floor. Making them go just where you want, simply by putting your paw in their path and herding them around the room, is a pretty good game.

Flies, of course, are more of a challenge, but I'm sure a hunter like you is ready for them, Fritz. Flies often get caught between the curtains and the window, and that's when they're the most fun. You need to sit on the windowsill and keep yourself very, very still. The fly sees you, of course (it has about a hundred eyes!), but when you don't move, the fly thinks you're one of those silly cat statues and that you'd make a safe landing strip. So it gets closer and closer. If you move quickly (and I know you can), you can squish that fly against the glass or simply snap it up in your mouth. Yum!

Spiders are great fun to play knock-hockey with, especially when there's another cat in the house. You both can lie down facing one another in the Sphinx position, and then toss the spider back and forth between you.

Check in the bathroom and the kitchen, around the cabinets and where the walls join the floors when you're looking for bugs. If you can't find any bugs, you can always sit and stare at the wall as if you have found a bug. Move your head around and pretend you're following its movements. Your person will keep looking and looking. Eventually, you can make his head move the same way yours does. This can be a very amusing game, so definitely give it a try.

You should also consider one of the home entertainment systems I recommended to BJ: the bird feeder. Because it's outside the house, Fritzie, you don't actually get to kill the birds. But this is not as frustrating as you might imagine. You still get to stalk the birds and sneak up on them. All cats have great imagi-

nations, so pretending to hunt can be a lot of fun. And if the bird feeder is right near the window, you can pounce against the glass and watch the birds scatter in terror. The best part is that birds are so dumb, they'll be right back at the feeder in just a few minutes.

And finally, every cat I know loves the furry mouse. Those tiny toys look and smell like real prey. And what could be better? They cost about a dollar apiece and last a long time. You can toss them up in the air, grasp them by the back of the neck, shake them, and kill them over and over.

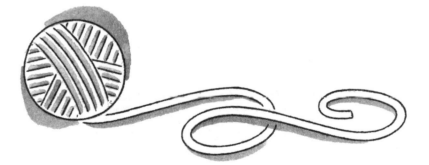

The Budget Toybox

Dear Tabby,

I love playing with my toys. I love stalking them, I love tossing them in the air, I love biting and shaking them, I love swatting and batting them. But what I especially love are new toys. They're covered with unusual smells, and I can pretend they're a kind of prey I've never seen before. Then I get to be a clever hunter and figure out how to attack them.

The problem is that my people don't have a lot of money to buy me all the new toys I want. They do take some of my toys and put them in the closet for a while, so when they come out again, they're almost like new toys. But not quite. They still smell familiar to me. I want more new toys, but my people can't afford them. Now what?

Your playful pal,

Chester

DEAR CHESTER,

How kind of you to think of your people's financial circumstances! Tabby says they absolutely must buy the best cat food there is and must never skimp on your veterinary care. But when it comes to playtime, clever people can take a cue from their clever cats. Even though I have a whole box of toys (plus a drawer full of other toys that I keep in reserve), I sometimes prefer to pull on a loose shoelace, swat around a hair clip, or pounce on a stray sock. My friend Yin Yin loves to sit on a pile of papers that are held together by a rubber band and snap the band over and over. (She is a very musical cat.)

Show your people what you like to play with by taking their things and batting them around the house. For example, if you like things that make a little tapping noise (like a mouse inside the wall), you might find a hard plastic ring or tag and drag it around on the linoleum floor. Do this often enough, and your people will eventually figure out that they can tie it to a piece of string and drag it around for you. If your people don't seem to be catching on, knock a piece of jewelry onto the floor and start batting it around. They'll notice!

If you like things that make a little rustling noise (like a mouse running through the grass), pounce on the newspaper whenever they are reading it. You can also roll around in the crinkly paper that comes inside the boxes they use to give each other gifts. Most humans catch on to this one pretty

quickly and will start crumpling up pieces of paper and tossing them for you.

If you like prey that flies or floats (like tasty poultry on
the wing), go under the couch or the bed and pull out some
fluff balls. All it takes is the slightest push to send those floating in the air. Jump at your people's clothes if they are wear-
ing swishy skirts or things with fringes. Show them how
much you like to chase toys that fly through the air. Eventually they'll learn to tie a little feather on a string for you.
Even a piece of toilet paper attached to a string and swished
through the air makes a nice flying bird.

Your people can make a sweet catnip toy for you from an
old sock. (Make sure you keep putting the other sock in the
dryer, so your humans can play one of *their* favorite games:
hunt for the second sock.) They can simply stuff the catnip in
the toe, tie a knot on the sock, and snip off what's left. An old
pair of nylons will
do just as well. They
can also poke the lit-
tle catnip bag into a
plastic whiffle ball,
which presents a bit
more of a challenge
for you, Chester. As
a matter of fact, cat-
nip is a very easy

plant to grow, and your people can usually find pots of it for sale in the spring at farmers' markets for a few dollars.

I have some feline friends who really like bubbles—the kids' kind you buy in a little plastic bottle for about 75 cents. They teach their people to sit on the floor and blow the bubbles gently across the room (*never* directly at a cat's face—how rude!). This is really easy for humans to learn, and they seem to enjoy it as well. (However, I do have at least one friend who thinks those floating bubbles are terror reigning down from the sky, and no matter how much I try to convince him otherwise, he just runs out of the room when the bubbles come out. Obviously, this is a signal to his people to just forget about that toy!)

Some cats like to chase a beam of light, but those laser toys aren't cheap. I just wait for my person to fall asleep in the afternoon with her watch on. Then I position her arm so the face of the watch catches the sunlight. It makes a circle of light on the wall that I can chase all afternoon. At night, your people can cut a round piece of cardboard to fit over the face of a regular flashlight, with a small hole in the middle. The very narrow beam of light that comes out is really fun to run after and pounce on.

Please remember to put away the small toys that you could chew up or swallow, the ones with strings or ribbons on them, and the feathery toys, when you're finished playing. Some other cat who is not as clever as you, my dear, could come by and swallow something he ought not to.

Catnip Bores Me

Dear Tabby,

    I have plenty of catnip toys, and I used to really enjoy them. They smelled fresh and sweet, and rubbing my face against them made me feel revved up and happy. I remember how excited I used to get as I inhaled that lovely scent, and then rolled around with delight like a kitten.

    But the thrill is gone, and these days even catnip bores me. Those toys just seem stale and old, and I've batted them under the couch and completely forgotten about them. I miss that old excitement, but catnip just doesn't do it for me anymore.

    Your fan in crisis,

    Isis

DEAR ISIS,

This is what happens when we lead a life of well-deserved luxury. Even the best things become boring. But catnip, that sweet, sweet herb, should always be something special for us.

Let me take a moment to talk about my favorite plant, *Nepeta cataria*. It makes us silly. It makes us roll around. It makes us happy. And then it makes us mellow, and we take a nice nap. It's all harmless fun.

Some cats, poor souls, never react to catnip at all. Kittens under six months are totally unimpressed (the silly little things!), and about a third of all adult cats remain indifferent to it all their lives. It's in the genes, you see, and some cats just don't have the catnip gene. (I suspect that's not your problem, though, Isis dear, since you said you have succumbed to its allure in the past.) For the rest of us, though, catnip brings us dangerously close to that line between dignified play and undignified foolishness. It is a line I, personally, have never crossed, but I know some cats who have. I will not name names.

The wonderful property that makes catnip the magic herb is an oil called nepetalacone that is concentrated in special glands on the surface of the leaves. When the delicate membranes around the leaves are broken, that heavenly aroma is released. One whiff, and it's a perfume advertisement come to life.

Did you know that our big cousins, the lions and tigers, also react to catnip? And our people do, too: Catnip tea makes them calm and relaxed.

Can we get too much of such a good thing? Yes and no. Catnip is safe and is not addictive. That's why you don't see tough catnip addicts hanging around people's gardens waiting for the plant to bloom so they can roll around in the buds. The only real danger from overindulging is that catnip loses its charm. And I suspect, dear Isis, that is what has happened to you.

The best way to overcome this little overindulgence is to lay off the nip for awhile. Put all your catnip toys away and don't think about them again for a few weeks. While they're waiting for you, store them in a plastic container or a glass jar to keep them fresh. When you're feeling like you really miss your catnip, take out one toy, crunch it around a little bit to release that lovely aroma, play with it until you're tired of it (which may be just ten or twenty minutes), and then put it away again. Bring the catnip toys out just once or twice a week, and they will always be exciting and special.

When you can't smell that minty fresh scent, even when you've crunched the toy a bit, it's time to toss it entirely and get some new catnip. Look for toys that smell really minty— not like grass or ashes. Even better is to have your people buy toys with reclosable pouches, so they can replace the catnip when it gets tired and worn. And they should never, never, never buy toys that say they are catnip scented or sprayed with catnip essence. They are *not* the real thing. And there's no point in faking it, is there?

Do I Look Like a Pro Wrestler?

Dear Tabby,

My problem is that sometimes my people like to wrestle, and wrestling is not a game I enjoy. I think they had a dog once, and that dog loved to roll around and wrestle with them. But Tabby, it must have been a big dog, and I'm the size of a Chihuahua; if they had a Chihuahua, would they have expected it to roll around and wrestle? I don't think so!

Meanwhile, sometimes they terrify me. They have this stuffed animal toy (I think it's a gorilla) that's almost as big as me. They tease me with it and poke it at me until I get so scared that I start kicking it with my back legs. I kick it because I want it to *leave me alone,* but my people think it's all a game. If I were a wild cat, I would never choose a prey animal that's as big as me, so this kind of wrestling is just plain scary.

Tabby, you and I know that we reserve the back leg kicks for fights with other cats. Frankly, I wouldn't mind a little wrestling with another cat, as long as it's all friendly, and we can call it off whenever we think things are getting too hot. We cats have clear body language signals that we all understand mean "I've had enough." But when my people poke me with that giant toy, I can't make them stop, and sometimes I really panic. I'm just not cut out to be a wrestler. I'm a lover, not a fighter. What can I do to make them stop?

Yours in need of protection,
Rocky

DEAR ROCKY,

You poor thing! You need a more satisfying and less scary way to play. I'm afraid one day you're going to get carried away and give your people a good bite. And sweetie, it won't be your fault if that happens.

Wild cats plan their attack before they pounce. Hunting and playtime are mental as well as physical, but your people seem to have pegged you for all brawn and no brains. How insulting!

Some cats respond to this kind of treatment by upping the ante and becoming aggressive. But I've never advocated biting the hand that feeds you, Rocky, so try a more passive approach. Simply ignore them when they start the wrestling match. Walk away if you can, and wait in a place where they can't reach you (try under the bed or in the back of the closet) until they get tired of playing with their stuffed gorilla. Make sure to walk away muttering, so they get the message. If they corner you, just crouch very low and hiss. If you don't make a game of it, chances are they'll get bored and give it a rest.

Meanwhile, I suggest you wait until they are out of the house and then urinate on the stuffed gorilla. Hopefully, it will smell so bad that they'll toss it out for good. And when you catch them watching wrestling on TV, step on the remote and change the channel. They need to learn about more peaceful pursuits.

Why Bother?

Dear Tabby,

I just don't like to play. It seems silly to me to chase and pounce on those little toys the humans give us. They're not real mice, after all, so why go through the motions of stalking and killing them? You always say a cat should be dignified, Tabby, and I agree wholeheartedly. And I am dignified just sitting on my pillows, keeping myself well groomed, and accepting the admiration of my people. I don't see why I should bother playing with them.

Your perfectly dignified,
Miss Puff

OH MY DEAR,

First of all, Miss Puff, I must tell you that playing is a very dignified feline activity. We show off our superior hunting skills to their best advantage when we play. Our people see how graceful, clever, and powerful we are. We tone our bodies and our minds. So don't be afraid to be yourself and have a little fun. We all need that.

Remember that play, for us, is like hunting. You need to get your person to play with you in ways that arouse the tiger in you. Toys that sneak around the house—fishing pole–type toys, sticks with feathers, and long trailing things—might intrigue you, especially if they move in mysterious, unpredictable ways. It's even better when they disappear under things, like a towel or a piece of paper. I really love the crinkly tissue paper that comes in the gift boxes humans give each other. When my person makes a feather stick disappear under it, the rustling noise is just like a mouse in the dry grass, and I go wild!

Toys should move away from you, not come at you (what prey animal ever runs toward its executioner?), and then slink around, sometimes waving slowly to tease you and sometimes barely moving to tempt you. And your person must be sure to let you catch the "prey" often, because if you don't have a successful hunt, why bother?

As I've said before, we cats watch our prey and plan the hunt before we ever pounce, so alert watchfulness all by itself is also a game. It may not seem that way, but when we look out the window, stare at the bird feeder, or watch our person dance around the house dragging our toys by a string, we're also playing.

Finally, you may not realize it, Miss Puff, but our people like to play with us. It's as entertaining for them as it should be for you. Your people are probably bored at night, stuck with nothing but the television and little containers of ice cream. They need you to get them off the couch and liven things up. They need your love and attention, your unending grace and dignity, and your inscrutable feline sense of humor.

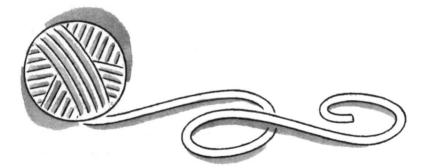

Litter Box Etiquette

If ever there was a bone of contention between cats and our people, the litter box is it. Our needs are simple: We want a clean box that's not too small, placed somewhere that's easy to get to and that helps us feel safe when we're in our most vulnerable position. Is this too much to ask?

But some of our people would rather pretend our litter box just doesn't exist. They hide it in cabinets, they stick it in corners, they forget to scoop, they buy litter that smells like dead flowers. Then they blame us when we refuse to use a dirty, smelly, inconvenient box. I've known plenty of people who are very picky about their bathroom habits, so why are they surprised when we cats are just as picky about our litter box?

It all comes down to understanding. If our people understood how sensitive our noses are, how it feels to stand in a box of litter with our soft little paws, how vulnerable we feel when we're getting down to business in the box, we'd all get along much better.

My People Never
Flush My Toilet

Dear Tabby,

My litter box is just too dirty to use. To
start with, it smells awful. Even my people
wrinkle their noses when they walk by it. But
they just put a cover on the box, stick a
charcoal filter in the top of the cover, and
pretend they don't smell a thing. I can't understand why they would want to live in a
house with such a stinky litter box. Meanwhile, that cover holds all the smell in, and
while the filter helps with the smell coming
out, it does nothing for me inside the box. If
they think it smells bad to them, they should
try getting into that box and standing just a
few inches above that litter! Sometimes I feel
like I'm going to choke.

I can't decide which is worse, though, the
smell or the fact that I have to pick my way
through a minefield to find a clean spot to do
my business. I'm lucky if they scoop that box
every two or three days, so the little piles
of poop are everywhere. I don't want to walk
on them! If they really don't want to scoop,

I'd be happy to bury my poop on the fringes of my territory, the way wild cats do. All I need is to find a good spot. In fact, I'm starting to think that pile of dirty clothes in the bathroom might be just the thing.

They want me to use the box, but then they make it the most unpleasant experience for me. Tabby, I am a pussycat with simple needs: I want my box scooped twice a day, and I want it thoroughly cleaned whenever it gets smelly. Is this too much to ask? What can I do?

Sincerely disgusted,

Lucy

DEAR LUCY,

What can you do? Go on strike, sweetie. In other words, stop using your box. Pick someplace clean and scratchable—a potted plant, a fluffy pillow, a sweater thrown casually on the floor—and use that instead. Your people may try to blame you for this, but it is most certainly not your fault. No cat should be expected to use a litter box that is not scooped at least twice a day and cleaned regularly—and many cats will not. No one can blame you, Lucy dear, if you don't want to use a toilet that is never flushed. It is absolutely unfair and entirely undignified to have to pick your way through an old, smelly mess to take care of a necessary bodily function.

Another strategy is to use your back legs to eject as many items as possible from your litter box. While your people don't seem motivated to scoop up these unpleasant things from your box, I guarantee they will pick them up from the floor. The only problem is that this will not take care of the liquid material, and that's what is really making your box stink.

Cats have twice as many scent-sensitive cells in their nasal passage as humans do, enabling us to smell things our people aren't even aware of. The implications are obvious. If your person can smell the box even a little bit, it's already overwhelmingly offensive to you. They've got to learn: It's time to clean it!

The Litter I Love Is Gone

Dear Tabby,

Can a cat love a litter? I'm beginning to think it's possible. The litter in my box used to be my favorite. It was soft like sand, and I could dig in it easily. It felt comfortable and inviting under my paws, and I loved to sift and sort it and bury things deep within it. Plus, it clumped, so whenever my people scooped, *all* the smelly stuff was removed, and my box just seemed fresher and more inviting.

But Tabby, that was all in the past. Nowadays, my people change the type of litter in my box every time they see a new television commercial or find a bag on sale. I get in the litter box, and it's always something new. Sometimes it's pellets that look like rabbit food. Sometimes it's clay bits. Sometimes it's little round balls in bright colors. Sometimes it smells like plants, sometimes like flowers, sometimes like perfume, and sometimes like nothing at all. I don't like surprises in my litter box, and I don't know how to tell my people to pick one kind and stick with it.

Longing for my litter,
Bert

DEAR BERT,

We cats are creatures of habit. It's not so much love of litter as it is love of routine. We get used to a litter, we grow accustomed to the way it feels under our paws, we learn to like digging around in it, we don't want a change.

Your people see an ad for something new, and they just can't help themselves—the company promises the litter is cleaner, sweeter, safer, ecologically more correct. They think you're going to love it, and they buy a bag. They're misguided, but they're doing the best they can. Love them, dear Bert. They love you. (Of course, this does not apply to people who simply buy the cheapest litter they can find. Those people need a quick lesson in economics: Any cat can completely ruin a rug in two days, and a new rug is a lot more expensive than a bag of better litter.)

Most cats (including me) favor a litter that feels soft like sand and smells like nothing at all. Bert, you seem to be a pretty easygoing guy, but some cats simply will not use a litter they don't like. Maybe the litter pieces are too big or too slippery for them to stand on easily and dig in happily. Maybe the litter pieces are too sharp to be comfortable. Maybe the perfume that smells so sweet to people makes cats want to gag. (Scented litter is just smelly litter in disguise— and it's not a very good disguise. The only way to keep a litter box smelling fresh is to scoop it twice a day and clean it regularly. You can't fool a cat's nose!) Whatever the reason, I know many cats who just will not use the box when they don't like the litter. Going on strike can be an effective way to communicate with your people. However, for the sake of peace in the house, I suggest a more subtle approach.

What you need to do, Bertie, is let your people know when you find the litter unacceptable. We all have personal preferences, dear, and you are entitled to yours. Go in the box, scratch around a little, and come right out with a puzzled expression on your face. Go back and forth, and look at your people as you come out. Make your face say, "Do you expect me to use this? Where is the litter I love?" If you have any bits of litter clinging to your paws, fling those bits against the wall with disdain. When your people are not around, scatter as much litter as you can all over the house so they'll think it tracks a lot; this will help convince them to switch. And if the litter has especially large or sharp particles, deposit a few pieces under the covers of their bed. After they roll over on it a few times, they'll understand how uncomfortable it is for you.

The Box from Outer Space

Dear Tabby,

My litter box is gone and has been replaced by a bizarre contraption that is filled with litter but that I know is not a litter box. I suspect aliens invaded the house one day when I was sleeping, grabbed the box, and replaced it with this machine. Whatever it is, it is far too strange for me to use. I went inside once to use it, and after I left, it started shaking and making noise. I almost jumped out of my fur! Who knows what will happen to me if I go inside again? I'm terrified, Tabby!

One really scaredy cat,
Smoky

DEAR SMOKY,

Ah, the ingenuity of humans! They have teams of scientists working day and night to invent litter boxes that people never have to clean. They have boxes that roll upside down, boxes with automatic rakes, boxes that flush like the watery litter boxes humans use (as if a cat would *ever* go into anything that gets sprayed with water!), boxes with trays people have to shake and rattle. . . . These scientists need to spend more time at home playing with their cats—and cleaning their litter boxes.

What's wrong with those "self-cleaning" boxes? Everything! To start with, most are way too small for a cat to get the job done in what I consider to be a dignified manner. We need enough room to leave a little something behind in several spots, yet still have a clean patch of litter to stand on.

They're also just, well, weird. They have moving parts. They make unnatural noises. They seem to have strange creatures trapped inside them. It doesn't matter that the moving and shaking and rattling happen when we're already out of the box—we still hear it, we know there's funny stuff going on in that box, and we feel it's wise to be cautious about ever stepping in there again. As you well know, Smoky, we cats are prudent creatures. The fancier the litter box, the less likely we are to use it.

A litter box is also one of the best ways we have of letting our people know we're sick. If they scoop it every day, they can see when something unexpected turns up. But if it's hands-off all the time, Smoky, you'll have to make those crucial deposits in a place where your people are more likely to see them. Perhaps the bathroom mat?

All those smart scientists, all that money wasted, when I could have told them there is just no substitute for scooping and scrubbing. Rather than forking out big bucks for those litter boxes from outer space, humans who simply cannot face a litter box would do better to spend their money hiring someone else to scoop and scrub.

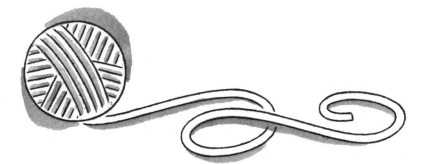

Where, Oh Where, Has My Litter Box Gone?

Dear Tabby,

My people move my litter box so often you'd think it has legs. They just can't make up their minds where they want it. It's been in at least a dozen places, including the bathroom, the hallway upstairs, and now the guest room--except when they have guests; then they put the box in the laundry room. Some of these locations are OK, and some are hard to get to, hard to find, or have too much going on around them. (I like a little peace and quiet when I'm in the box--is that too much to ask?)

I don't like having to go hunting for my litter box as if it were a scampering mouse. Sometimes I wake up after a nap and can't remember where the box is, so I just go to the last place I remember and pee there. How am I supposed to keep up with this litter box relocation program?

Puzzled about where to pee,

Patches

DEAR PATCHES,

With litter boxes and real estate, location is everything. Your people need to sit down and think hard about where they want the box, choose a place that is acceptable to them and you, and then leave that box where it is—*forever*.

Let's talk a little bit about litter box locations. You mentioned the bathroom, and this is not a bad idea. The box is easy to clean, easy to find, and easy for you to get in and out of—as long as it's not in the bathtub, wedged behind something, or "hidden" inside the vanity under the sink. (Humans leave their toilet bowl out in full view, so I don't know why they're so picky about seeing our litter box!) After they take a shower, the litter can get pretty damp, though, so it's important to leave it uncovered. Your people also need to make sure the bathroom door is open *all the time*—even when guests stop by.

What about the basement? Bad idea! First of all, no one is going to remember to clean your box when it's down there. And anyway, basements are dark, damp, scary places far from your family. They're full of junk that can fall and hurt you, scare you, and convince you never to go in the basement again. People are *very* particular about where they go to the bathroom, and they'd never put one of their water litter boxes in a place like that.

Anyplace where there's a lot of noise and people coming and going is a bad idea. So the playroom, the den, the kitchen are all out. As you yourself said, Patches, we cats like a little peace and quiet when we're in the litter box. It can be a challenge for your people to find a balance between the "no-cat's-land" of the basement and the population density of the rumpus room, but there's no way around it. Litter box location is important, and they'll just have to work at it.

The laundry room might be a better choice. That's a warmer, nicer room, and your people will be in and out, but not too much. Some kitties get scared, though, if they happen to be in the box when the spin cycle kicks in. If you are one of these sensitive souls, Patches, the laundry room is a bad choice for you.

The middle of a hallway, off to the side at the top of the stairs, or the corner of a quiet room are excellent choices. Anywhere near your food and water dishes is not. No self-respecting cat will eliminate near his food and water supply. It just isn't dignified.

Our wild cousins eat at home and then walk to the edge of their territory for a pit stop. Why do they do this? Because they are clean, fastidious creatures, of course! But also because it's safer not to leave strong scents near where they and their kittens live—scents that hungry predators are only too happy to read like a map. So here's a question for your people: If there's only one place to get food (the food dish), and if the litter box is nearby, will a cat give up the food, or will he just find another place to use as a litter box? This is not a hard question!

One more thing to remember: People like to have a bathroom on every floor of the house, and so do cats.

Another Missed Opportunity

Dear Tabby,

I'm a big orange tabby boy, and I like a big litter box. My person is very good at accommodating me. I have a big open box in a nice spot in the corner of the hallway, and he keeps it scooped and clean. I want to show him how much I appreciate his efforts, so I'm always careful to go in the box. Even when I feel like spraying to assert myself, I do it in the litter box.

The problem is that despite my best efforts, I sometimes end up peeing over the edge of the box or on the wall. I'm a big boy, Tabby, and I don't squat like a girl when I pee. I want to be nice to my person, but what can I do?

Sincerely (sorry),

Sonny

DEAR SONNY,

I am glad to hear your person is trying hard to make sure your litter box is as inviting as possible. And Sonny, you set an example for all cats by rewarding good behavior from your person with good behavior of your own. This is certainly a dignified way to behave. Tabby approves!

Of course, these little mishaps are not your doing. The answer is a new litter box. Some boxes come with a cover, but I don't think that's going to work for you, Sonny dear, because you're such a big boy. Some cats do fine with a covered box (extra large size, of course), but you're likely to bump your head on the ceiling. And if every time you go to the litter box you get a knock on the head, how long will it take for a clever boy like you to learn to stay out of the box?

No, covered boxes generally don't work for the big boys—or for those cats who prefer not to squat when they get down to business. The best solution for a cat like you is a tall plastic storage box. You'll have to send your person to a home supply store to get one, rather than a pet supply store. Unfortunately, this means he will not come home with a bag of treats and a new toy for you. However, he still has to go to the pet supply store for litter and cat food, so this shouldn't present too much of a hardship.

Anyway, leave the top off your new skyscraper litter box, so it doesn't get too clammy and damp in there. Of course,

I'm not expecting you to leap in the top every time you need to use the box. No, no! Your person must cut a U-shaped hole on one of the narrow ends of the box, so you can easily get in and out.

The tall sides will keep your pee contained. This means it won't be on the wall or the floor—a good thing. But it also means your person will have to clean the box more often and make sure he scrubs the sides. If he complains, remind him that it's better than scrubbing the wall.

Too Tiny to Reach

Dear Tabby,

I'm a kitten who recently moved away from my feline family and into the home of my new people. Mostly I like them. They play with me a lot, and I have a soft little snuggly bed to sleep in, interesting toys, and plenty of good food--and I don't have to fight with my brothers and sisters for a place at the food dish, either.

The one thing I don't like is my litter box. It's nice and clean, and they did show me how to use it. My first few days here, after every meal my people put me in the box and scratched a little with their funny-looking paws, and I got the idea right away. They were so proud of me!

The problem is that the sides of the box are really high, and I have a hard time climbing in and out. When I wake up after a long nap and have to go, it seems like almost more trouble than it's worth to scale the sides of that box. I'm just a little kitten, Tabby, but they expect me to climb Mt. Everest every time I have to pee. Now there's talk of moving it into the bathtub. I'll never get in and out of there! But I'm afraid if I don't use my box, they won't keep me. Help!

Your tiniest fan,

Karma

DEAR KARMA,

Someone has forgotten what a tiny thing you are, my little Karma kitty. Soon enough you'll be able to run with the big cats, but not yet. Your people just aren't seeing the world from your low-to-the-ground point of view.

It's not fair to expect a kitten to scale the sides of a giant litter box—much less the slippery walls of the bathtub. You need a litter box with lower sides, and you need it put in a place that's easy for a little kitty like you to get to. When you're a bigger boy and can easily hop in and out of boxes twice your height, they can bring that big litter box back out and put it where they like.

You have two weapons at your disposal right now, little Karma. The first is your impossible kitten cuteness—which you should play up as much as possible, because, believe me, it won't last long. The second is your ability to appear truly pitiful because you're still somewhat skinny and have a squeaky voice. Use these to your advantage.

Go right up to the edge of the litter box, sit down, and look up at your people. Meow in your squeakiest, most pitiful voice. Make your face say, "Help me! I want to do the right thing, but I can't." When they ask you what's wrong (and believe me, if you get the meow right, they will), make a pathetic attempt to climb into your box, but—and here's the key—be sure to fail. Pull yourself up to the edge with one paw and then fall back onto the floor and pretend you're hurt. (Don't worry, because you won't be. All kittens are made of rubber and simply bounce or roll when they stumble.) Lay it on thick, sweetie. They'll get the message. If they don't, pee on the floor as close to the box as possible. Show them you're trying, but just can't reach.

If you were an adult, Karma kitty, all this whining might be considered undignified behavior. But for a kitten, it is perfectly acceptable. In fact, eliciting pity is an important survival skill for all young animals. Tabby says: Use it 'til you lose it!

I also think you need to help your people understand what it's like to be such a little kitty. Try to get them down on your level more often. Do this by knocking their things onto the floor. Do not knock over things that will break, because this may make them angry (if it does, meow pitifully and look as cute as possible—you might even pretend you've scared yourself—and they'll forget it in a second). Stick to objects made of plastic and metal, and you'll be fine. When your people bend over to pick them up, prance over and start to play. Tug on their shoelaces, swat at their earrings—whatever it takes. The idea is to keep them down on the floor, so they can begin to see the world from your perspective.

Staking Out My Turf, Part I: Intruder Alert!

Dear Tabby,

Lately some tough cats have been coming into my backyard, spraying the outside of the house, walking past the windows, and generally invading my territory. Even though I don't go outside, that space around the house is mine-- the edge of my turf--and a guy's got to protect his turf. I can see them out the window and sometimes can even smell where they've sprayed, so I spray the wall under the window in retaliation.

I *need* to leave a mark to let them know this is my territory. I know you understand this, Tabby. But my people don't. They get really upset every time I spray, and they claim I'm messing up the house. Why aren't they proud of me for defending our home turf?

One truly tough cat,

Max

DEAR MAX,

First of all, cats should not be roaming around in your backyard. As I've already discussed in Part Two, caring humans simply do not put their cats out of the house to roam around like wild animals. We are *house* cats! Those roaming invaders need to be neutered and kept indoors, where all self-respecting cats belong.

However, we can't control the behavior of humans we don't live with (unfortunately—can you imagine what we could accomplish if we were able to?), so those roaming rascals are not likely to disappear. And if they do not, Mr. Max, you have every right to stake out your territory and defend it against intruders.

What your people are not understanding, sweetie, is that for cats (in fact, for most animals except humans), urine is a form of communication—a smell-o-gram, if you will. You're not messing up the house, you're messaging the world.

You have done your part to keep the intruders out of your territory. Now your people must do what they can. They can start by erasing the smell-o-grams those delinquents have left behind. Around the doors and windows are the favorite targets of those graffiti artists, but your people should sniff all around the house for smelly messages left behind. Then they should get out the hose, a scrub brush, and some bleach, and go to work.

A persuasive word with the neighbors about their

roaming cats is a good idea. Tell your people to mention the word "lawsuit," because humans seem to really fear that word. A tall fence might also work. If that's not possible, your people can at least line the areas right up against your house with things cats do not like to walk on—gravel, pinecones, chicken wire, dogs—so these marauding feline miscreants will not get up close and personal.

Blocking your view might also be a good idea, because most cats live by the motto, "If I can't see it, it isn't there." Just the lower half of the windows is enough. They can put up pictures of fierce tigers and panthers, so the invaders know you mean business.

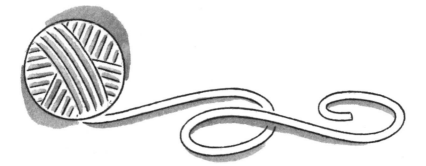

Staking Out My Turf, Part II: Bully at the Box

Dear Tabby,

   There are four cats in this house and only two litter boxes. No matter how often my people scoop, the boxes get really messy really fast. But that's only part of the problem. I don't like having to stand in line to go to the bathroom, and I don't like other cats hanging around while I'm in the box, meowing at me to hurry up.

   We all have preferences, too. Snuggles, for instance, prefers to pee in one box and poop in another. But because the rest of us aren't so selective, she can never find a box that is "uncontaminated" with the wrong kind of stuff. (Snuggles is a very picky girl in other ways, too; she won't let anyone sniff her behind, for example. Go figure!)

   Then there are the access battles, and these can get pretty ugly. Watson thinks he's the dominant cat in this house, and sometimes he just stands guard by a litter box and swats at anyone who tries to use it. Or he'll ambush Pearl when she's in the middle of doing her thing. Sometimes he waits halfway down the hall, and when you come out of the box, he runs at you and starts a fight.

The litter boxes are both wedged into corners, and the one in the bathroom is turned so you can't even see who's coming--which means you could be ambushed at any time. It makes all of us pretty nervous about using the litter boxes, and sometimes we don't. I mean, I just can't take care of business with all that anxiety!

For myself, I've selected a place in the house that I consider to be safe. It faces the entrance to the room, so I have plenty of time to see Watson coming. It's also in an open area, so I have several escape routes to choose from. Usually I can just dodge around him and sprint to another part of the house. This is the perfect place for me, and I use it almost all the time. The problem is that it's on a rather nice rug, and my people seem to be upset about this. How could they think their rug is more important than my safety and peace of mind?

Definitely nervous,

Nellie

DEAR NELLIE,

Life for us is all about territory, and access is just another part of the ongoing feline turf wars. Access to food, litter boxes, the best spot on the couch, the warmest parts of our people—that's a big part of the feline lifestyle. Sure, we groom each other's ears and lie down together on the bed, but even cats who get along can suddenly find themselves in a stare-down. We never stop defending our place in the pyramid.

I'm sure Watson's defense of his top spot creates a lot of anxiety for Snuggles, Pearl, and you. If it makes you feel any better, I can assure you that he's feeling pretty anxious himself, having to assert himself all the time. I know from firsthand experience, it's not easy being Top Cat. (Honestly, did you think I would accept any other position?)

Your people are lucky Watson isn't spraying the outside of the litter boxes (and any other upright surface he can find), because that's a typical tactic for macho guys like him. The rug is easy to deal with: They need to send it out to be cleaned. If you've been using it as your private litter box for a while, this is definitely a job for the pros.

As for the relative worth of a cat and a carpet, Tabby says no contest! Does a rug snuggle up with you on cold nights? Does a rug soothe you with gentle purring? Does a rug welcome you at the front door with tail held high? Does a rug rub against your legs to reassure you that you are part of that carpet's territory? Rugs don't even *have* territory! Plus, they're made from the hair of shedding sheep, and sheep are very stupid animals. Need I say more?

Meanwhile, your people should be learning from you, little Nellie, about what cats in a cat pack need when it comes to the delicate issue of litter box etiquette. First of all, with four cats they need at least three litter boxes; three boxes, no waiting. If the house has more than one floor, they need at least two boxes on every level (that's four—the price your people must pay for wanting a bigger house).

They can't all be crowded in the same area, either. If Watson is guarding the litter box area and all the boxes are close to each other, you have the same old problem, don't you? If they are spread out around the house, though, you and your sweet sisters can each find a litter box that is safe to use. You can step in, relax, and get down to business.

To make sure you can easily plan your escape route, the boxes shouldn't be covered, wedged in a corner, stuck in a closet, or hidden inside those silly cabinets that are supposed to fool people into thinking the box is a potted plant. People are actually not that stupid. They cannot disguise a litter box, so why try?

Having lots of boxes is no excuse to ease up on the scooping, by the way. Nothing—and I do mean

nothing—will ever change the fact that every box must be scooped twice a day and scrubbed whenever it smells. That, my dear, is one of the absolute truths of life.

No cat can be expected to use a litter box if it gives her an anxiety attack. We all need a little peace and quiet when we are in that most vulnerable position. And we need to know we're not trapped in the bathroom; it can spark some close-quarters fighting that a cat never wants to get into. It is never, never dignified to fight in a litter box.

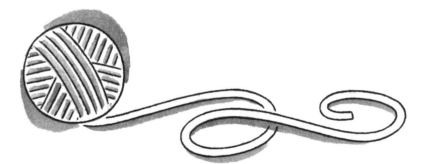

When Peeing Is Painful

Dear Tabby,

    I've decided to pee on the bed. I've made this decision because lately every time I pee in my litter box it hurts. Obviously, something has changed in my box that is causing me this pain, and if I just stay out of the box, I think I'll be fine. The problem is that my person, Richard, really doesn't like me peeing on his bed. Is there a solution?

    Painfully yours,

    Foxy

DEAR FOXY,

Oh sweetie, it's not the box! I can see why you've come to that conclusion, but Foxy honey, you've misunderstood the situation. You've probably got a urinary tract infection—they're not uncommon in cats—and you need to see a veterinarian right away. These infections can become very serious if they're not treated, so don't wait another day.

Listen up, cats and kittens, because this is important. If you feel the urge to pee all the time, but when you go in your box it hurts and there's not much urine, or you're feeling uncomfortable "down there" and need to lick yourself a lot, or you're getting sudden urges and feel like you don't have time to make it to the litter box, these are all signs that you are sick. They are not signs of hostility on the part of your litter box. In fact, your box is an innocent bystander in all this.

After your vet finds out what is causing your pain and helps make you all better, you may need some gentle urging from Richard to get back to using your box. We cats are quick learners, but sometimes we learn the wrong lesson. It may take you a little time to unlearn the idea that your box caused your pain.

Richard needs to clean up every place where you've peed with a special cleaner that has enzymes that eat up all the urine molecules. (The cleaner is easy to find at those great stores that have miles of aisles of cat food and toys.) I'll bet he thinks he's already cleaned and that all the smell is gone. But you, my dear little Fox, can probably still smell that distinctive *eau de cat*, and it will only encourage you to pee in the same places again.

After the cleaning, it's a good idea to make sure you can't revisit those old peeing grounds. Covering them with a piece of tin foil, a plastic shower curtain, or carpet runner with the nubbly side turned up will help keep you focused on your litter box when you need to go.

Now, as for peeing in Richard's bed, I understand why you did it. And it's important for him to see that you are sick so he can take care of you. But, sweetie, you can't blame him for getting a little upset. You wouldn't want him to pee in your snuggly little bed, would you? The next time you're feeling sick and need to give Richard a message, try peeing in the sink. It's much easier to clean up.

Getting Old and Harder to Hold

Dear Tabby,

My litter box is upstairs at the end of the hallway. It's always been there, and I've always been happy with it. It's easy to get to as well--if I'm upstairs.

But I'm getting old and I just can't hold it like I used to. If I'm sleeping in the sun downstairs and wake up and need to go, it's a long climb for me all the way up those stairs and a long climb down, and I can't always wait. I don't often feel like hiking up those stairs, either.

There's a big potted plant down on the main floor, and the dirt in the pot is starting to look pretty tempting to me. Our ancestors buried their waste in the dirt, so it would be a perfectly natural thing. Any thoughts?

Old and bothered,
Belle

DEAR BELLE,

Let us take a moment to consider the graceful lives of older cats. They sit in the sun like the Great Sphinx, immovable but still impressive. They seem to know everything, and they certainly tolerate nothing. I can't think of anything more dignified than an older cat, and it's up to our people to do all they can to help us preserve our dignity as we age.

Older cats like you, dear Belle, get stiff joints that make it tough for them to climb up and down stairs and in and out of a litter box. Kidney problems, diabetes, and other diseases can increase their urine output and make it harder to get to the box in time. They have senior moments, too, when they forget where the box is. And loss of muscle tone just sometimes makes it harder to hold.

The first item on your agenda, supreme Miss Belle, is to take a trip to your veterinarian and make sure your health is fine. Whether you're healthy or not, though, the solution for you is more boxes. You need one on every floor of the house, and they should be in places that are comfortable for you and within easy reach of where you like to sleep and survey the world. The boxes should be uncovered and have low sides, so you can step in and step out like a lady. If you really have a hard time getting around, plastic trays—the kind your humans use in a cafeteria or fast-food restaurant—may be a better choice. They have to be cleaned very often, but darling Belle, you are definitely worth it.

Older cats don't like the cold, either. (Well, no cat likes the cold, really, but older cats like it even less.) So if a litter box is in a chilly basement or garage, it should be moved someplace warmer. It is disrespectful to expect an older cat to use a cold litter box. And if a cat has been going outside to do her business, she may decide one day that it's too darn cold to go outside anymore. Her people must respect this decision.

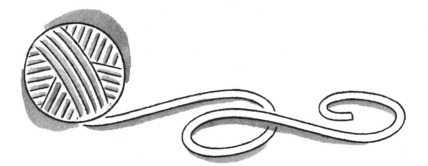

PART 4

Scratching, Hissing, and Other Uncouth Behaviors

Humans and felines have different values. For example, when a human looks at a brand new sofa, she sees a fine piece of furniture, sturdy and made to last, covered with a stylish fabric that goes perfectly with the decor of her living room. When a cat looks at a new sofa, she sees a fine scratching post, sturdy and made to last, covered with a rough fabric that is perfect for sinking her claws into.

Conflicts arise because cats see the world very differently. OK, we're not always perfect. But we're not mean or spiteful, either. We have good reasons for everything we do. It's just that our people don't always understand our reasoning.

Climbing the Curtains: Because They're There

Dear Tabby,

Climbing the curtains makes me feel like the Top Cat. I love scampering up them as fast as I can, then using my claws to cling to the top as I survey my territory. I'm the big jungle cat, looking out on my kingdom. When I get excited, climbing those curtains is always the first thing I want to do. It's such a great way to use up all that energy!

But my people don't seem to share my enthusiasm. They yell at me whenever I start scampering up the curtains. And lately they've taken to squirting me on the back with a water pistol. This is so rude, I just can't believe it! Why don't they want me climbing the curtains? Do you think I'd be better off climbing up the china cabinet?

Your curtain-climbing kitty,

Sherpa

DEAR SHERPA,

Humans live their lives in two dimensions: forward and back, side to side. Maybe they stand on a ladder to change a lightbulb, but they feel uneasy up there and get down as soon as they can. We cats, on the other hand, are three-dimensional creatures. Up and down are as natural to us as left and right. Our ancestors climbed trees, and we still can. In fact, we have very special organs in our ears than enable us to know exactly where we are in space—like super feline astronauts—which is why we almost always land on our feet. We are exquisitely *designed* for the high life.

When we are up high, we feel safe and secure. We're not afraid of falling (we are far too graceful and poised for that!), and we love having an overview of our territory. From the high ground we can see exactly who is coming and going, we can't be surprised, and no one can sneak up on us. For our ancestors, that panoramic view was a matter of survival (many of them ate their meals in trees so they would not be disturbed), and for us it helps us feel at ease.

That said, there are certain realities of life we all must accept when we live with humans. One of them is that people have certain things in their homes that they would prefer we do not damage. I know, my little Sherpa, it is difficult to accept the possibility that not everything in your home is your personal property. But there are certain concessions we must make to our humans, because, after all, they buy the food and the litter, they pay the heating bills, they play with us, and they're nice to sleep with.

Certainly, your intention is not to damage the curtains. You just want a place to climb and have some fun, and you like the view from up there. But your clutching little claws, those same efficient weapons that enable you to cling to those curtains like a fly on the wall, also pull and tear the fabric. And shredded curtains are not what humans have in mind when they think of home decorating. For that same reason, I'd stay away from the china cabinet. They probably like most of the things in it and don't want to see them broken.

We really have two problems here—yours and your humans'—but it's easy to solve them both. First, your people should consider switching to a type of window dressing that's not quite so tempting for you. Venetian blinds are one possibility, although I do know several cats who insist upon climbing those as well. This is a very bad idea, because these cats tend to get hopelessly tangled in the blinds, which is extremely undignified. Vertical blinds are almost impossible to climb, and many people who live with cats have found them to be an ideal solution.

While your people are making their home-decorating decisions, they can control your urge to

surmount the drapes by tying up the ends so you can't get started on your little expeditions. Tying up the drapes isn't exactly the most fashionable way to display them, but your people will have to make a decision about what is most important to them.

That may solve your humans' problems, but it doesn't solve yours, dear Sherpa. You need to climb, and you *must* have somewhere you are permitted to do so. In fact, if you have a super climbing spot, you may decide to abandon the curtains entirely—tempting as they may be.

I have heard of people who completely redo their homes with high ramps and walkways, so their cats can dwell far above them. This, of course, is the ideal solution and one I wish more humans would adopt. But we must be realistic: Few people are willing turn their homes into feline jungle gyms.

Many people will clear out the top shelf of a bookcase for an intrepid feline, and for some cats this is all they need. However, it is certainly not too much to ask that every feline household have a multilevel cat tree. Is it unreasonable to expect that we have just *one* piece of furniture in the house that is ours to do with as we like? Absolutely not! We need to rest in high places, and if our people don't want us resting on their tall furniture and their curtains, they must give us furniture of our own. The higher we like to climb on the curtains, the taller the cat tree must be. For you, my climbing Sherpa, a floor-to-ceiling model may well be the answer.

Since your eye-in-the-sky perch is supposed to be a place where you can survey your territory, it should be in the room where you spend the most time, placed near a window so that you can carefully watch the world, inside and out. The well-made cat tree also doubles as a scratching post, playground, and snuggly bed, so this is the wisest sort of investment a human can make.

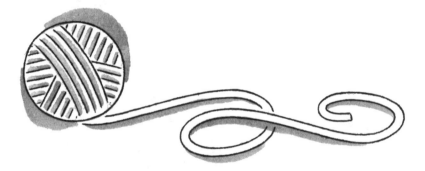

Desperate for a Good Stretch

Dear Tabby,

My person has brought home a ridiculous scratching post that I simply cannot use. First of all, it's entirely too short. When I take a nap, I spend hours sleeping in a tight little ball, so when I wake up, I want to sink my claws into the top of something tall and have a good stretch. I need to arch my back and loosen up all my muscles. But with this short thing, I can barely stretch out the kinks in my spine. Plus, when I put all my weight on it, it wobbles and wiggles like it's going to fall over. I'm itching for a good stretch, but I just can't scratch.

That post is totally useless as a nail groomer, too, because it's wrapped in cushy carpeting. I like to sleep on that stuff, but I don't like to scratch on it. I've been reading your advice for years, Tabby, and I know you always tell cats to avoid damaging their people's furniture, but I have to groom my nails and I have to stretch, so I have no choice but to use the arms of the sofa.

My person, of course, yells at me and makes loud noises and does other things to scare me when I scratch the sofa. She once even put balloons on the sofa arm, and I nearly jumped out of my fur when one of them popped. Lately I've been so nervous. My nails are a mess, and my nerves are shot!

All shook up,

Elvis

DEAR ELVIS,

So many times a cat tries to do the right thing, but his person just doesn't understand what he needs. Every cat needs to scratch and needs the right kind of surface to do it on. You can't be blamed for seeking a suitable scratching surface. No wonder you're all shook up!

It's really a shame when people go to the cat supply store full of good intentions and the store sells them exactly the wrong thing. Yes, those same cat supply stores, the ones with miles of aisles of fabulous cat food and treats, also sell scratching posts that no self-respecting cat would ever lay his claws on. They're made to look cute—maybe they even have a funny little toy sticking out of the top—but they're not designed to help a cat get down to the business of scratching.

Let's take a moment to reflect on what cats in the wild scratch. Trees! What do we know about trees? They're tall. They're rooted deep in the earth. They're hard and rough on the outside. These are all clues.

So what have we learned? As you mentioned, Elvis, we need a scratching post that's tall enough for us to stand up on our back legs, anchor our front claws, and get a good stretch. We cats are long animals, so we're talking about a pretty tall post. (Here's an interesting little fact about your slinky spine: The discs between each vertebra are cushier and thicker than they are in humans, which means we actually get a bit longer when we jump to a far windowsill or shelf—

or when we stretch. In other words, even little cats need tall scratching posts.)

A tall post needs a wide base to keep it from wobbling or falling over. This is basic mechanics we're talking about—an idea humans should be able to grasp easily. When they're looking at posts in the store, they should try the push test: If they push on the thing and it wobbles, it's going to wobble when you push on it, too. And if your scratching post wobbles, why would you use it? Especially when the sofa doesn't wobble.

Now when it comes to your manicure, sweetie, all dignified cats take this very seriously. Your nails grow in layers, and when the inner layers grow, the outer layers need to be pulled off. Your scratching post must be wrapped in something rough that you can really sink your claws into, because when you pull them out again, the loose outer layers of the nail come off easily. They look like beautiful little silver crescent moons, which you can leave artistically arranged around the base of the post.

For a proper manicure, many cats prefer a scratching post wrapped with rope or a rough, scratchy fiber called sisal. Some even like a post made of hard wood, like a tree trunk.

If your person has pieces of leftover carpet lying around from the last time she redecorated, you can demonstrate your preferences by turning the carpet over and scratching on the rough back side. This may help her understand exactly what kind of surface you really need to scratch on (since, clearly, your scratching the couch has so far not taught her anything). In fact, people with tall but soft scratching posts can simply recover them with a piece of leftover carpet turned backwards. The money saved can then be spent on extra treats and toys for their cats.

Now, I do know some cats who like to scratch the rug. But this is not because they crave the cushy surface; it's because they like to scratch horizontally. If they had a choice, they'd always choose one of those horizontal scratching pads wrapped in rope or made of corrugated cardboard. In fact, we cats deserve one of each: a vertical post and a horizontal pad. If our humans anticipated these basic scratching needs—and met them—we'd have no need (or desire) to shred the couch.

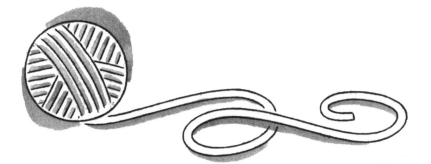

Can't Scratch in the Dungeon

Dear Tabby,

My person recently went out and bought me a state-of-the-art cat tree for a scratching post. I mean, this thing was loaded with features: three and a half feet tall, two different posts with different surfaces, two curved shelves and a little tunnel, a base that's wide and heavy--this baby has it all. It's big and it's beautiful.

My problem is that he decided it's too big for the living room and stuck it in the basement. Now he expects me to do all my scratching down there. But Tabby, I barely even consider the basement to be my territory. It's dark and smelly and chilly, and the only time I even go down there is to investigate when I think I hear a mouse running around.

I actually like that post better than the table leg I'm scratching on now, and I wish my person would bring it upstairs.

Longing to scratch in public,
Dante

DEAR DANTE,

Remember what I told Patches in Part Three about litter boxes? Location, location, location. It's true of scratching posts as well. We like to scratch when we wake up, and cats just don't sleep in chilly basements.

The basement is about the worst place I can think of for a scratching post, but the guest room, the laundry room, or anyplace else where a cat and his people seldom hang out is also a bad choice. Think about it: Are you going to wake up from a nap in the living room and walk all the way down to the basement or into the laundry room for a good stretch and scratch? Not likely! Any cat will probably just anchor his claws in the back of the comfy chair.

In addition to stretching and that all-important manicure, scratching is also a marking behavior. In other words, we use it to indicate important parts of our territory. The scratches provide a kind of visual signpost that says, "I live here!" (That's another reason why we like to reach up when we scratch; a signpost that's way up high says, "The biggest cat you can imagine lives here, so don't mess with me!") We also have scent glands on our paws that leave behind a message only other cats can sniff.

The thing about marking, dear Dante, is that it's only worth marking the really important parts of our territory—and those include prime napping and viewing areas and access points to important rooms. So, for example, we might feel the need to leave a mark at the end of a long hallway, right where it opens up into the living room. Marking access points is most important to cats who live in multicat families, but even cats who live alone need to mark their territory. You just never know when another cat is going to wander by, and you need to be ready. Cats are *always* prepared.

We also scratch when we're feeling frustrated or excited. So we might want to scratch when our person comes home (we're happy to see him, after all), when he's busy fixing our dinner, or when we run into the room ready to play. If there's no scratching post handy, we're going to start carving up the table leg. But no self-respecting cat gets excited about anything in the laundry room or the formal dining room. What goes on in those places? Nothing!

We like to be where our people are, so that's where our scratching posts and cat trees should be as well. The living room or TV room are good choices. The bedroom is a nice place for an extra cat tree, too.

Now, as for your human thinking the cat tree is unattractive in the living room, I cannot even imagine such a thing. There is no question in my mind that a well-designed, well-made cat tree is the most attractive piece of furniture in any home.

What's "Declawed," and Is It Bad?

Dear Tabby,

I'm a kitten, and I just arrived a few months ago at my new home. When I was a little guy, I really had trouble controlling my claws, and sometimes they'd be out when I meant to have them in. They still get caught on a lot of things, and sometimes I accidentally scratch my people when they use their fingers to play with me. I don't mean to, but my little claws are very sharp, and I have a bit of trouble controlling them.

Sometimes I get very excited, too, like when I'm running from one room to another, and I stop and scratch on the rug or the couch. I mean, I'm trying to be good, but it's not always easy. And I know I'll have better control of my claws when I get a little older.

Lately I hear my people talking about having me declawed. I'm not sure what this means, but I don't think I like the sound of it. What's your opinion, Tabby?

A nervous kitten,
Kaboodle

DEAR KABOODLE,

Your little kitten instincts are correct. Declawing is a bad thing for cats, and I strongly urge you to refuse to have the procedure done.

Let's start by thinking about why we need our claws. Of course, they are the supreme samurai swords when we have to defend ourselves. A cat who goes outside without her claws might as well be naked. But even cats like me who live indoors need our claws. We use them to grasp and manipulate our prey, our toys, and our food. We use them to help us get our footing, to grab the surfaces we jump onto so we don't fall (which would be *very* undignified!), and to steady and balance ourselves as we spring, run, climb, and stretch. We can't leap gracefully and we can't get a good stretch without our claws. We also use our claws to express ourselves: When we're sitting beside our people, purring, content and happy, we move our claws in and out and scrunch up our paws. This is a very dignified way for a cat to show her love.

So why do people want to declaw their lovely little cats? I think it's because they don't really understand what's involved, and they're not sure there's an alternative to having all their furniture carved up into garden mulch. We cats need to educate ourselves about declawing so we can help our people understand why it's not a good choice.

Dear little kitten Kaboodle, this explanation may be a bit hard for you to read. The realities of declawing get rough in spots. But I promise, after the tough stuff, I will explain how you can learn to scratch only what your people want you to scratch.

Now, young Kaboodle, you may have looked at your people's hands and thought declawing is like humans losing their fingernails. They'd have nothing to paint and file and chew when they're nervous, but it might not be so bad. The problem with this thinking is that our claws are nothing like human fingernails. They are part of the last bone in our toes, and when a cat is declawed, that entire last bone must be removed. It would be like cutting off the tips of a human's fingers at the last joint.

If this sounds painful, it most definitely is. Declawed cats generally feel a great deal of pain and require pain medication for five days or even more after the surgery. Some cats develop infections and other serious problems.

The very thought of this gives me nightmares. But it gets worse. When that joint is removed, the sensory and motor nerves are cut, and they do not repair themselves for many months. During the recovery time, whereas a person might be sitting with his feet up or hobbling around on crutches, a cat has to keep walking over to his food dish, scratching in his litter box, jumping onto and off of the bed. Plus, a declawed cat must learn all over again how to walk, run, and leap minus half of all the toes on his front feet.

I have seen very sweet cats change after being declawed. Some become aggressive when they realize their primary defense weapons are gone. They figure the best defense is a good offense, and they bite at the slightest little thing. Some cats feel pain in their feet for the rest of their lives and become sulky and depressed. Some never really feel graceful and beautiful again and lose their feline spark. Others turn shy or timid. They've had their toes cut off, for heaven's sake!

I do believe that when our people understand exactly what declawing is and how it affects us, they will agree that we have the right to keep all the toes we were born with. But to be fair, cats and kittens, we must also agree that people have a right to have nice things in their houses—things that we don't recarve and redecorate with our claws.

Kitten Kaboodle, I promised I would explain how you can learn to control your scratching behavior. So let us begin. First, as I've said before, all cats need to scratch, so you need the right kind of scratching post, put someplace where you would want to use it. I've just explained all this to Elvis and Dante, so I won't repeat myself.

Next, you need to unlearn your bad scratching habits and learn some good ones. Your people will have to help here. The best way to unlearn a behavior is to make it totally unappealing. Cats simply will not do anything they don't enjoy. So all the places you really love to scratch now—the table leg, the arm of the couch, the back of the cushy chair—

need to be covered with something no self-respecting cat would *ever* scratch. Smooth plastic is especially repugnant, so a tarp or shower curtain might be a good choice for the sofa or the chair. Plastic car or shower mats can be thrown over the sofa arms. Aluminum foil is also particularly nasty. Of course, people usually don't like to sit on these things either, but it's only short term.

Double-sided tape will also keep you away from the good furniture without having to cover it up. There's a brand called Sticky Paws that is safe for most furniture and can be washed off with plain water. Your people can just stick it on the spots where you like to scratch. And if there's a big area they want to make off-limits, they can use the tape to stick down a cover so you can't wriggle up underneath. I personally found Sticky Paws to be very persuasive when I was a wild young thing.

Your excellent scratching post should be placed right in front of the sofa arm or comfy chair, or wherever you like to scratch. (If you're a horizontal carpet scratcher, a scratching pad should be set right over your favorite spot on the rug.) This way, when you go to your familiar spot to scratch, you'll find the nice furniture covered with something nasty and a fabulous scratching post just waiting for you to sink your claws into. Your people can rub the post with some enticing catnip, too, so it seems like the best place on earth to scratch.

If you're still not getting the idea about where to scratch

(and I don't mean you *personally,* sweetie, because you seem to be a clever kitty), a little playtime near the scratching post will help. Since we tend to scratch when we're excited, this encourages a cat to try out the perfect post. I have heard about people who put their kitties' paws on the post to demonstrate, but this is just scary and will not teach a cat anything except not to let his person grab his paws. Cats learn by watching, so your people can scratch the post a little themselves, just to give you the right idea. I have always found this to be very entertaining and amusing.

We cats are very smart, and it doesn't take us long to figure out where to scratch and where not to scratch. In just a few weeks all those mats and shower curtains can go back in the closet, that awful sticky tape can be thrown away, and the scratching post can be moved (gradually, of course) to a better spot in the living room.

There may still be times when we get so excited that we run into the room and scratch the first thing we see. A quick distraction with a toy is the best way to break up this unauthorized manicure.

Hang in there, Kaboodle, and try to keep those claws under control!

The Counter Cruiser

Dear Tabby,

My people like to cook, and they're always spreading delicious food all over the kitchen counters. They do all kinds of chopping and mixing and fussing with it, and then cook it up in ways that make fabulous smells dance all over the house. I love to watch them handle the food, and sometimes they give me a little piece, so I hang out with them whenever they're in the kitchen (when I'm not taking a nap, of course).

Sometimes when they're cooking, they leave food sitting out on the kitchen counter for a while, and I think in those situations it's OK for me to jump up and have a taste. After all, they've left the food out and uncovered, right? But my people don't seem to agree. Whenever they see me on the kitchen counters, they yell at me. I can't understand why they're doing this--they leave the food out where they know it's no problem for me to get it, and then they yell at me when I do. What's up with that?

I've realized, though, that I can outsmart

them at this game. If I jump up on the counter, take a quick bite or two, and then quickly jump down, they never catch me at it, and I can taste everything. Plus, I've discovered that even after they clear away all the food, there are still delicious little tastes and smells that linger on the countertops all the time. So I just wait for them to go out or go to bed, and then jump up and explore as much as I want.

So far this has been working pretty well for me, but do you have a better idea for how I can get even more stuff from the counters without being yelled at?

Your cool counter cruiser,

Minke

DEAR MINKE,

When food is involved, it doesn't take very long for a clever cat to outsmart his people. The next step for you, my little food thief, is to learn how to open the refrigerator. I wouldn't bother with the kitchen cabinets, though, because they're full of dry, grainy things like pasta and flour. There may be cans of tuna in those cabinets, but I've never yet met a cat who can work a can opener. (If you do figure it out, you *must* write me immediately!)

I know how tempting unattended food can be, dear Minke, and it is completely unfair of your people to expect you to sniff a large roast of beef or an open can of sardines on the counter and not try to eat it.

Still, I worry about you, because dangers may await you on the kitchen counter. People use knives to cut up their food (they don't have teeth that are designed to rip meat off the bones, the way we do), and sometimes they leave those knives on the countertops. They also sometimes leave the tops of cans up there, and while lids may be very yummy to lick, they have sharp edges that can cut your tongue. Humans also eat foods that are not good for you and can even make you sick, such as onions, chocolate, and alcohol. You're a curious boy, Minke, and if you eat too much of these things, it could be a disaster.

Plus, there might be breakable things or pans that are very hot on the kitchen counters. You're jumping up onto a surface you can't see, and you might knock something over that smashes on the floor or burns you. When you jump back down, you could be running through broken glass.

Still, Mr. Minke, you can't be expected to simply refrain from your counter cruising—especially not when your people occasionally offer you yummy bits of food from the counter-top. Self-control is most definitely not a feline virtue. No, it is the responsibility of your people to make sure they do not leave anything dangerous behind. That means putting all the knives away and leaving no glassware or hot pots unattended.

As for your question about getting more, I think it's best to stick with the plan you've already worked out and limit your countertop explorations to times when your people are either in bed or not at home. It's less likely something dangerous will be left out, and you stand almost no chance of getting caught.

Just be thankful you don't live where my friend Yang Yang lives, because he has some particularly sneaky humans who have convinced him to stay off the counters for good. The key to their clever plot was to set up a situation where he had an unpleasant experience every time he jumped up on the counter—*whether they were home or not.* I can hear you howling out there, Minke, and I want to tell you about how they did it so you'll know what to watch out for.

First, they got together some things cats don't like to walk on: aluminum foil, cookie sheets filled with water, bubble wrap, plastic car mats with the nubbly side turned up. They put one out on each counter, so when Yang Yang jumped up, he found himself standing on a cat-hostile surface and jumped off immediately.

But here's the really dastardly part: They left that nasty stuff on the counters all the time. So poor Yang Yang was stuck with a sort of remote-control correction. Every time he jumped up on the counters he had an unpleasant experience, even if his people were asleep or away from home. Now he never goes up on the counters, even though his people sometimes don't put out those cat-hostile items. And can you blame him? The way he figures it, he's more likely to find an uncomfortable situation up there than he is to find a tasty treat.

Fortunately for you, Minke, such deviously clever humans are rare indeed.

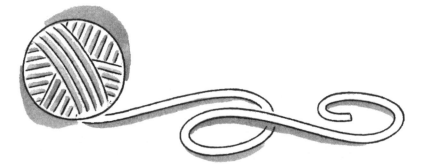

Where's My Salad?

Dear Tabby,

Like all cats, I'm a meat eater. Show me a mouse, and I'll rip its head off. I like a good, meaty cat food, too. But as a side dish I really like to have a salad now and then.

My problem is that all my people ever put out for me are houseplants. They're pretty to look at, but they don't really taste good, and my people seem upset when I eat them (if they don't want me to eat the plants, why do they put them out?). What do you do when you crave some greens?

Looking for greener grass,

Otto

DEAR OTTO,

Here's an interesting little fact: Feral cats who must feed themselves select plant matter for about 10 percent of their diet. Nobody is really sure why, but it may have something to do with a desire for roughage to help with digestion, a need for some of the vitamins in plants, or simply a craving for something fresh and green. Do we need to know exactly why we like everything? No. It's enough that we like it and want it. As far as I'm concerned, that means we've got to have it.

There are a few problems with eating houseplants, though. The first, as you've learned, is that people actually form attachments to their houseplants. They *like* them and get upset when they're destroyed. I do not want to even begin a discussion of the psychology involved here; just accept my word that this is true.

The other problems are more serious. Houseplants, at their most harmless, simply taste bad. At their worst, they can kill you. And somewhere in between those two extremes, they can upset your tummy and make you throw up. It all depends on the plant, of course.

Centuries ago, our ancestors learned about horticulture the hard way. Some panthers were walking along, and one of them stopped to munch on a plant. A few minutes later, he fell down dead. The next time they saw a plant like that, the mother panther probably told her kittens, "Don't ever eat that plant! It killed your Uncle Pete." Knowledge like that got passed down through the generations.

But these days our indoor moms don't need that kind of knowledge, so they can't pass it down to us. And anyway, humans bring home plants from all over the world. We can't possibly be expected to know which ones are poisonous and which are not. In fact, most humans don't even know that information.

Even the plants that are not poisonous can be dangerous. Maybe they're sprayed with something to keep away the bugs. Maybe they have some kind of fertilizer on them that is very bad for cats. Maybe they have stuff sprayed on them to make their leaves shiny or their flowers brighter. Maybe they're in heavy pots that will knock you on the head if you accidentally tip them over (don't tell me you don't swat at the trailing leaves, Mister, because I know you do!). Plants may *seem* like harmless salad, Otto, but they can turn into killer greens.

So what's a cat with a craving for salad to do? Well, first of all, your people need to help you stay away from the houseplants. They should be hung on hooks or put on very high shelves where you absolutely can't reach. And I'm sure an agile boy like you can get to a lot of places in your house, so your people need to think carefully about this. They can also try spraying the leaves with a bitter-tasting (but harmless) liquid such as vinegar or one of those taste deterrents they sell in cat supply stores. (Do you find it disappointing—I know I do—that the stores that sell aisles and aisles of delicious cat food, yummy treats, and fabulous toys also have things like taste deterrents?)

This keeps you out of danger, Otto, but it still doesn't get you what you want. Cats who crave salad must have some. I know cats who eat a little plate of chopped lettuce every day. However, some of us demand that our greens be *au natural,* and that means our people must plant some just for us.

Those very same cat supply stores also sell little kits of what they call "cat grass." Usually it's a mixture of wheat and oat grass, and the seeds come planted in a little pot. (Or your people can buy the seeds and a separate pot, plus some sterile potting soil.) Your people give the seeds some water and then put the whole thing in a dark closet until they sprout. When the grass starts poking through the soil, it's time to put the pot in the sun. Now you have your own houseplant, Otto—far tastier than the stuff your people have been growing and perfectly safe. Chances are you will choose it over your people's other plants every time.

There are some things to remember, though. I am sure

that you, dear Otto, are the soul of moderation, but not every cat is. Some cats graze like sheep (I am not entirely convinced that this is a dignified activity, but am reserving judgment for now), ripping the grass up by its roots and killing whatever they don't eat. So they may need a little grazing time each day, and then the pot can be tucked back into a safe growing spot. Or their people can keep several pots of grass growing at the same time; grass won't make us fat, and, as we know, humans can never overindulge their cats' desires.

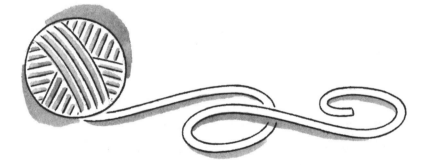

Too Much Heavy Petting

Dear Tabby,

I like to be petted, but only up to a point. At first it's usually nice, but after a while I've just had enough. The problem is my people keep petting me even after I've made it clear that I don't want them to. And sometimes they touch me on my rump, which I don't like, or on the belly between my back legs, which I absolutely cannot stand.

I tell them when I've had enough, but they just don't understand when to stop. So then I have to hiss at them or slap their hands or even give a little nip. I don't break the skin, and I let go as soon as they stop moving their hands, but really, I don't like to bite them. There seems to be no other way to avoid all this heavy petting, though. What do you suggest?

Let's (not!) get physical,
Ariel

DEAR ARIEL,

As you know, I firmly believe you must never bite the hand that feeds you. But you also have the right to be left alone when that is what you want. We all adore physical closeness from our people, but we want it on our own terms. While we have been living close to them for hundreds of generations, we just can't seem to shake out all those tiger genes. And tigers are not longtime cuddlers. So sometimes we want a snuggle, but soon the tiger takes over, and we've had enough closeness, thank you very much!

Let's stop a moment and look at this from two points of view. You, dear Ariel, have sat down next to your person for a friendly cuddle. Your person pets you for a while, maybe starting under your chin or behind your ears (which I know all cats simply adore), but then she begins to move down your back and starts ruffling the fur on your rump. This is something you simply cannot abide (and frankly, my dear, neither can I!), and you send off several little signals that tell her so. You are patient and keep trying to tell your person that you have now reached your petting limit. But she just doesn't listen. So you quickly turn around and take a swipe. Perfectly justifiable, as far as you're concerned. But let's go inside the mind of a person for a moment and look at that same little scene.

Your person sees sweet Ariel sitting down for a cuddle. She pets you in your favorite spots and sees that you like it.

She figures more is better, and keeps petting. She's probably doing something else while she's petting you, such as watching television or reading or talking to someone. Suddenly you whip around and take a nip at her. What happened? Her feelings are hurt—and maybe her hand as well. Yes, dear Ariel, this really is how people see the world.

First, ask yourself, are you *sure* you're letting your people know when it's time to stop petting? Think of all the signals cats use to make it clear they've had enough. Some are very subtle, and when it comes to reading body language, people are in the first grade, while we cats all have Ph.D.'s. So rotating your whiskers forward, for example, may not even be noticed by your people. Even if they do notice, I doubt they'll realize this means you're heading into prey mode. They don't know that rotating our whiskers forward is a sign that we are ready to go on the offensive (because we cats can't see very well directly in front of us, we use our sensitive whiskers to get a lot of information about prey that is close to our faces).

Your people may notice but simply not understand certain signs of feline irritation that would be a dead giveaway to another cat. Twitching your skin is a good example. When horses twitch their skin, it means they have a fly crawling on them. When people do it . . . actually, I believe people can't twitch their skin at all. So how can you expect them to know that it means you are annoyed by their attentions? Putting your ears straight out to the sides or laying them flat back are also common signs of feline annoyance. But people never talk with their ears—they only listen with them—so they may not get that message either. Some cats simply shift their weight, but again, this is just too subtle for most humans.

You may have also tried staring or looking back at them several times (I imagine your face says something like, "What is wrong with you? Can't you see I've had enough?"). A pointed look is one kind of body language people do use, so they ought to understand it. If you combine your staring with something very obvious, such as swishing or thumping your tail, they really have no excuse for not getting the message, and they should stop petting you immediately. If they don't, then under these circumstances you must administer a correction. Your people *must* be trained to pay attention to you when you are trying to communicate.

However, I advocate gentle training methods, and I believe you should always start with the lowest-level correction. That means a verbal reprimand. A low-pitched growl is a good attention getter. It is a foolish human who ignores a low-pitched growl, because this is a noise that says, "There's more to come if you don't listen now." I absolutely believe when a cat growls, her human must recognize it for the reprimand it is and not take it personally. We cats have the right to growl in what we consider to be extreme circumstances. It's a form of communication.

If your growl is ignored, follow it up with a hiss. I cannot even imagine a human who does not understand what a hiss means. However, your people still may not be able to put it all together. "OK, Ariel is annoyed," they might think, "but what have we done?" They still may not understand that they've been petting you too much. This is when I believe a swat correction is perfectly permissible. A quick slap on the hand is all that's required—and *claws in* please, Miss Ariel, because you don't want to hurt them.

Now, some of you may be thinking, "Why doesn't Ariel just get up and walk away?" But dear felines, I absolutely must take her side in this argument. Our people are warm and soft and comfortable, and just because we don't want to be petted doesn't mean we don't want to be near them. Certainly, we have the right to be near them without being stroked to the point where we become irritated. And finally, our people do need to be trained to understand our language. After all, we listen carefully to them. It's not too much to ask that they listen carefully to us.

I Like a Little Bite
Now and Then

Dear Tabby,

Sometimes I just feel like biting. I don't know what comes over me, because I actually like my person very much. I'm not angry with her, and I'm not a mean cat. I'm not even sure why I do it. If my person just stops moving her hand, I let go right away--that's all it takes. Still, this is not good for our relationship. Do you think there's something wrong with me?

Noticeably nippy,

Nina

DEAR NINA,

Certainly, you don't sound to me like a mean-spirited feline, and I'm sure you are not. There are many reasons why a cat may bite, dearie, but you were not specific about what the circumstances are when you decide to get aggressive. So to clarify things, I will explain the reasons why cats bite, and perhaps this will enable you to understand why you are behaving this way.

Know thyself, Nina. I certainly hope this information helps you control thyself, as well, because, as I've said many times, a cat should never bite the hand . . .

To start with, Ariel has just explained how too much petting can cause a perfectly nice cat to nip. Petting on the tummy, closer to the back legs, will also earn a bite every time. This is a feline survival instinct (an attack in the tummy area would quickly be fatal), and it has served us well for thousands of years. You absolutely cannot be blamed for biting anyone who pets your tummy in that reflexive bite spot. He or she should have long ago figured out that cats always bite when touched there, and *stopped touching you there!*

A lot of feline aggression is related to playtime. After all, for us playtime is hunting time. And hunting time is when we kill things! We get pretty aggressive with our toys, biting and kicking them and throwing them in the air. If your person is using her hands as a toy to play with you, you can't be expected to know when the game has stopped. A toy is *always* fair game, and if you've learned that fingers are a toy, fingers are always at risk for a nip. Rough play also inspires the gentlest cat to bite—simply in her own defense. (Remember Rocky the reluctant wrestler in Part Two?)

The solution here is for your person to keep her distance from your toys when you're playing. Toys on sticks or on strings are great fun, and there's no chance you'll mistake a finger for a furry mouse. If you like little toys, you can play games where your person throws them for you, rather than holding them in her hand—where they are, after all, an extension of her ever-tempting fingers.

If you've already gotten the idea that fingers are fine playthings, it's not much of a leap of logic to assume ankles are, too. Maybe you lie in wait behind the couch and pounce on your person's ankles when she passes. This train of thought is easy to follow: Toys are like prey, prey moves, my person's body is a toy, my person is moving . . . ankle pouncing, of course, comes next.

In my experience, Nina my dear, most ankle pouncers are simply bored. They're not getting enough playtime. Several active games every day—using toys that your person does not hold close to her—should help burn off that extra energy.

Are strange cats creeping around outside in your yard, circling the edges of your territory? That is an intolerable

situation and one that sometimes causes cats to bite our humans. Of course, we know perfectly well that our person isn't the invader, so how could we make such a terrible mistake? Well, Nina, when we see those miscreants outside taunting us, possibly even peeing on the periphery of our home turf, we just want to get out there and rake them with our claws. We get annoyed, we get agitated, we get wild. We can't engage those wandering delinquents in combat, but we're in a state where we're ready to bite the first thing that comes near us. And we do. It could be a person, the family dog, or even another cat. The poor victim is left wondering, "What did I do?" and you're still lashing your tail and wishing you could tear the ears off those cats outside.

The best thing to do in those cases, Nina, is simply be by yourself until you've calmed down. Your person can help by keeping the wandering strangers away from your door. (I have already explained how to do this in my answer to Max in Part Three.)

Sometimes cats bite because something has scared them and they feel cornered. Are you a timid girl, Nina? Maybe you've taken a nip out of your person when you're on the way to the veterinarian or when there's a repairman running an electric drill in the kitchen and you just want to hide in the closet. Scaredy cats give very clear signals that they need to be left alone. Their pupils get big and round, they press their ears flat against their head, and they may even hiss or growl.

What they're really saying is, "Leave me alone!" I believe it's always prudent to honor that request.

Cats also bite when they're hurt. A cat who has been in a serious accident or who is trapped in some painful way will lash out at anything near her that is moving. Obviously, this is not your problem, Nina. But perhaps you have a touch of arthritis or an ongoing pain elsewhere, and whenever your person touches you there, you instinctively defend that tender spot with a bite. This is how our ancestors protected themselves, and it's how we do, too. Our instincts are part of us, and we can't deny them. If you've always been a good-natured girl and have suddenly found yourself being crabby and nippy, it's time for a thorough checkup. Please try not to bite the veterinarian.

I Hate the New Cat

Dear Tabby,

Recently my people brought home a new cat--
an invader in *my* territory--and now this hot-
shot is trying to take over. His name is Rudy,
and I think that's because he is so rude. We
fight all the time, and the stress is really
ruining my coat.

Sometimes he hides at the end of the hallway and pounces on me when I try to go into
the family room. I just want to sit and watch
TV with my people, but mean old Rudy won't let
me pass. We get into stare-downs that last for
minutes, until somebody throws a punch. Sometimes he even stalks me around the house, so I
can't sit down quietly anywhere. I hiss and
swat at him, but then my people think I've
started the fight and make me leave the room.
This is so unfair! This guy comes into *my*
house, and now *I'm* the one getting blamed for
the violence. How can I get rid of him?

At the end of my rope,

Lola

DEAR LOLA,

When felines fight, things can get ugly. We have many ways of expressing hostility, ranging from stalking to staring to scratching. Intimidation is a language we understand fluently. It's all extremely stressful, and it can quickly escalate into violence.

We can be a touchy species. I have seen two cats sleep together peacefully on a chair, then wake up and immediately launch into a slap fight. We have proximity issues, OK?

We also have dominance issues, and you, Lola dear, seem to still be working those out. When a new cat comes into another cat's territory, either he acts very submissive, or he tries to take over. Rudy sounds like the pushy type. These bullies chase other cats away at playtime, try to scare them from the food dish, harass them in the litter box, push them off the sunny spot on the couch, and maintain control over key routes in the house. That's why Rudy lays in wait for you at the end of the hallway—to keep you from safely entering the coveted family room.

Your people don't understand that the cat who hisses is usually on the defensive, and by chasing you away they've let Rudy think he has staged a successful coup. They need to take that big boy down a peg or two, so their first rule should be that whenever a fight starts, it's the aggressor who gets banished. The next time Rudy stalks you, tries to block your way, or engages you in a stare-down, they need to step between you and then calmly put him in another room for a brief time-out. When he comes back, you should be sitting in one of the best spots in the house, just to show him you're not going to act the victim for anyone. Hold your ground if he tries to chase you away, and make sure your people back you up on this.

At playtime, have you been hanging back and letting Rudy swat at the toy? One piece of prey is not enough for the both of you. Your people should play with you separately, but also schedule some playtime together using two toys. This way, you don't have to compete for the prize, and you both can learn to relax while playing together.

Look around at the key paths you and Rudy use to get around the house. Is there a narrow hallway where you simply can't avoid bumping into one another? Do fights mostly take place in the doorway leading into the kitchen? As I said before, we have proximity issues, so if there is any way your people can make those areas a little bit less cramped, perhaps by moving some furniture or setting up a little ramp, they should do it.

Adding more territory is also helpful, since you both probably feel you need your space. The ideal would be to build you each your own wing of the house, but if this

is not practical, a multilevel cat tree is a less radical alternative. Vertical territory is as good as horizontal, I always say.

If hostilities escalate to the point where you two simply cannot be trusted together, the best solution is a fresh start. You and Rudy need to be separated for a few days, and then reintroduced slowly and carefully (in Part Five there's a letter to the divine Ms. Diva that explains how to properly introduce two cats).

When you start interacting again, it should be quick and from a distance. Maybe you both eat on opposite sides of the same room, and then are once again whisked away to your neutral corners. Build up your tolerance time slowly. I am a big believer in bribery in these situations: Play, treats, catnip, and other goodies should always be around when you're together.

You and Rudy may never be best buddies, but these tips should at least help you tolerate one another. Even though most cats develop a kind of natural hierarchy, it should not turn into a dictatorship. Your people should never let Rudy bully you—especially at mealtimes or in the litter box. If that means you get your own litter box and they have to be the food police, so be it. You were there first, Lola, and you deserve some consideration!

The Feline Guide to Surfing the Internet

Dear Tabby,

My person Heidi recently started working at home. I thought this would be a positive development in our lives—more playtime, more lap time, right? But she spends a lot of her day working at her computer and not enough playing with me. I do sleep on her lap sometimes, and that's pretty nice, but eventually she has to get up to go to the bathroom or get a cup of tea, and then I have to start my nap all over again someplace else.

I try to get her to pay more attention to me by walking back and forth in front of the computer screen, but that just makes her mad, and she picks me up and puts me on the floor. So then I decided to take a look at this computer and see what's so fascinating about it. And actually, it's pretty cool! There are words and sometimes even pictures that appear and disappear and move across the screen. Then there is the keyboard, which clicks and rattles. (I love the sound, but Heidi absolutely refuses to let me type on the keyboard. She

says it messes up her work--how insulting!)
And finally--you're not going to believe this,
Tabby--there's a little hard plastic thing
that Heidi calls a *mouse*. It's nothing like a
mouse at all! But it's still fun to swat
around the desk.

The problem with all this is that the more
interested I am in the computer, the more annoyed Heidi gets. She never lets me use it,
and she seems to give it more attention than
she gives me. What can I do? I'm . . .

Fed up with that mouse,
Cookie

DEAR COOKIE,

As I mentioned in Part Two, we must allow our people to work so that they can buy us superior cat food, litter, and toys. In any case, I advise all cats to sit quietly and watch while their people are using the computer, because computer skills are something every cat should have.

Cookie, you may see that misnamed mouse as just a silly toy to be batted around, but in a knowledgeable paw it can become a gateway to every cat's dream. I am talking, of course, about the Internet. I think the Internet must have been invented by genius cats, because it provides us with a perfect opportunity to secretly interact with the human world. Nobody ever sees your whiskers on the Internet, and you don't have to speak, so you can pretend to be human.

You may be wondering why any feline would want to pretend to be human, but on the Internet, dear Cookie, if you're a human, you can *shop*. I'm talking about tons of the finest cat food, always in your favorite flavor, whatever toys catch your fancy, the biggest and best cat trees—anything you can think of, you can buy on the Internet. And it will be delivered right to your door!

My advice to you, sweet Cookie, is to watch Heidi very carefully when she's working at the computer. Sit quietly on her desk and look interested. A time will come when she stops typing and pictures start appearing on the computer screen. That's the Internet. Watch carefully how she uses the mouse to get into and out of the Internet. It's just a few swipes, and then you press the silly little mouse with your paw. A clever cat can learn how to do it in just a few days.

Now here is the crucial part: Never, never, *never* let Heidi know that you can access the Internet. This must be our secret. So don't jump up on the desk in excitement and grab the mouse out of her hand when she starts to use the Internet. Just sit quietly, or, even better, pretend to be bored and take a nap on top of her computer. The only time a cat should ever use the Internet is when his person is asleep or away from home.

You will need one more thing for shopping, Cookie, and that is a credit card number. Fortunately, I am sure Heidi can provide this for you. Chances are when she pays her credit card bills she throws the old bill in the trash can. Watch carefully the next time she does this, but wait until she goes to bed before you retrieve it. Remember, this is a secret! The bill will have her credit card number, and that's all you need to buy things on the Internet.

Now you're ready. When Heidi goes to sleep, simply turn on the computer and go onto the Internet. You're ready to shop. Love those tuna treats? Order a case of them.

Want a fleecy new window perch? Get the fancy kind with the built-in heater. See some fun feather toys you might like? Order a dozen. The Internet has everything! Simply use Heidi's credit card number when you're ordering, and everything will show up at your doorstep in a few weeks.

Heidi will never know why all those boxes of cat food and toys are being delivered. But when they are, remember to thank her and act as if it were her idea. Rub up against her and make your face say, "I love you so much for buying me all these wonderful things." Then give her an extra long snuggle in bed to show your appreciation.

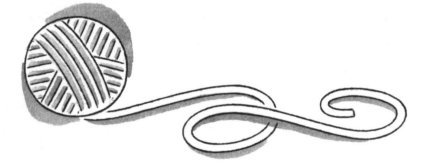

PART 5

It's OK to Show Affection (And Get Attached)

We felines have been the victims of some absurd myths and a few sad ones: for example, that we don't form attachments with our people and that everything we do is motivated by a desire for food. I don't know how these myths got started, but I do know they're untrue. I have seen poor affection-starved cats walk away from a full bowl of food so they could sit in a friendly lap and be scratched under the chin. And any person who has had a cat follow him into the bathroom in the middle of the night knows how attached we get to our people. When it comes to people and cats, the more we understand each other, the more we trust each other. And out of trust grows love.

Are You My Mommy?

Dear Tabby,

My person reminds me of my mommy. My mom was big and warm and snuggly. My mom was always looking out for me, trying to teach me things and keep me out of trouble. My mom fed me from her nipples, and then later brought me food and taught me how to eat it. She groomed me when I got scruffy and purred to me when I felt scared. When I slept snuggled in against her, I felt warm and safe.

My person does a lot of those things my mommy used to do for me. She feeds me and grooms me and plays with me and keeps me out of trouble. She holds me and cuddles me. When I sleep next her head at night, it's warm and safe like sleeping next to my mommy.

I know my person really isn't my mommy, but she makes me feel so safe and happy that sometimes I treat her like my mom anyway. I like to snuggle up next to her or get on her lap and press my paws against her and move them back and forth, because that's how I used to make milk flow from my mom's nipples. Kneading my person like that is very comforting and it

makes me purr. Of course, I don't drink milk
from my mother anymore, but the kneading reminds of when I did. So sometimes I like to
suck on my person's shirt when I knead. I especially like to snuggle up under my person's
arm and do this, because I like the way she
smells there.

I'm not a kitten anymore, but snuggling
and kneading and suckling still make me purr
like one. Do you think it's undignified?

Still a kitten at heart,

Smudge

DEAR LITTLE SMUDGE,

There is absolutely nothing wrong with a little kittenish behavior. Thank heavens we live inside these days and no longer have to take everything in life so seriously! Even grown cats enjoy a good cuddle, and we all love to snuggle the way we did with our mothers.

Many people also enjoy a good snuggle. Snuggling is relaxing, warming, and soothing for everyone involved. I believe cats—and people—who snuggle live longer, happier lives.

For your person's sake, though, please keep your nails trimmed. When you knead, those little claws go in and out. It's one way we express our pleasure, but re-member that our people don't have fur on their skin to protect them.

Now, as for the suckling, some people don't mind it, Smudge, but many of them do. Among people it's consid-ered undignified to walk around with a wet spot on their shirts. And I have seen cats get so worked up over their trip down childhood's memory lane that they start to drool. Def-initely undignified!

Cats are born knowing how to suck (how on earth would we survive those first few weeks if we weren't?), but our mothers must teach us to stop. Your person can do the same by very gently (and I do mean gently!) closing your mouth or simply tickling you on the chin whenever you gather up a mouthful of clothing and start to suckle. If she puts her arm around you at the same time, you can still enjoy the snuggle without the mess.

Don't worry about showing your attachment to your new "mommy," Smudge—just be sure to be sensitive to her feelings, too.

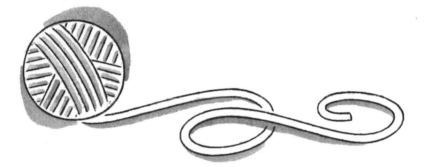

All I Need Is Love

Dear Tabby,

I think of myself as a typical cat. I spend part of my day sleeping in the sun, part of it eating, part playing, and part surveying my world in a dignified manner. I like to watch my people, and I like to play with them and pet them, too--but when I'm ready. I'm not always in the mood for a cuddle, and I don't like to be picked up or forced to sit in some-one's lap. But that doesn't mean I don't want to be petted. I just don't like the loss of control that comes with being off the ground or in a lap. I don't think that makes me an unfriendly cat.

The problem is that my people assume I'm aloof, so they act aloof with me. But all I really want is some love. Is it so bad to want to be alone sometimes? Does that mean I have to be alone all the time?

I feel so misunderstood,

Morty

DEAR MORTY,

I have a theory about aloof cats: Aloof people end up with aloof cats. Why is this? Because we cats are perfect mirrors of the people we live with. We are generous, loving, devoted creatures, but only with people who are generous, loving, and devoted with us. We give of ourselves what we get from others.

This is yet another way in which we are different from dogs. Dogs love the people around them boundlessly, even if those people don't give their dogs much attention in return. This is not because of some flaw in dogs (now, I hear some of you hissing, and you must stop; dogs are dignified in their own way—it's just not the same way cats are dignified), but because dogs have always lived in groups or packs. In the wild they are almost never alone, so it's their nature to socialize with anyone, any time.

But we cats evolved as solitary hunters, and we socialize with whom we choose, when we choose. We are not programmed by our DNA to be pals with every creature who comes along. Unfortunately, our role as solitary hunters has created a myth that we are solitary creatures, and this is just not true. The comparison with tigers, who live most of their lives alone, goes only so far. In reality, we love the company of others. Stray cats with no people to keep them company form little packs of their own. They still hunt alone, but they groom and play and sometimes even raise their kittens in groups.

We definitely have times when we'd rather just be left alone to sleep in the sun, but we love affection and always give as good as we get. Still, people hear that myth that cats are independent and aloof, and they make it come true by treating their cat as if he doesn't need or want affection. The cat then stops looking to them for affection, and they say, "See, I was right. Cats are aloof. They don't love anyone."

Morty dear, you have a particularly generous heart because you are looking for love from people who don't show you how much they love you. They probably don't understand that while you sometimes prefer to be left alone, that's not *always* what you want. Not everyone feels snuggly every moment of the day, and it's OK for you to have your moods. But if your people prefer a pet who *never* needs any loving attention, they're better off with a tank of fish.

What can you do? Keep trying to show them what you need. Sit next to them on the couch and put a paw on them. This will show them there's a way to be close without your feeling like you've lost control. Follow them around the house. Just being in the same room with them is a way

of saying, "I care about you." During quiet moments at home, look deeply in their eyes and make your face say, "I wish you understood how much I love you." When they pet you, try to give them a lot of positive reinforcement by purring and closing your eyes.

By all means keep things on your terms, and when you need to be by yourself, take your quiet time. But if you encourage them to show you more affection when you approach them, you may find yourself approaching more and more often.

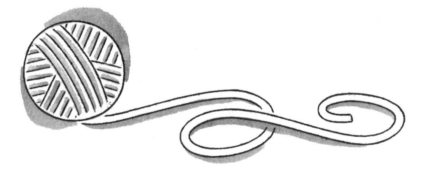

Sleeping Alone Stinks

Dear Tabby,

    I really like sleeping with my person. She's warm and snuggly and smells familiar and nice. Sometimes she lets me sleep with her, and she seems to enjoy it, but sometimes she closes the bedroom door and won't let me in. I assume she's forgotten to leave the door open, so I meow very loudly and scratch at the door to let her know I'm out here and waiting to come in. But she doesn't seem to hear me.

    Sleeping alone is cold and boring, and sometimes I feel uneasy during the night. If I could just be with my person, I would feel so much better. But I'm afraid she's becoming more and more forgetful about leaving the bedroom door open, or else she's going deaf, because she doesn't seem to hear me meowing. What can I do?

    Your frustrated friend,

    Freddy

DEAR FREDDY,

First of all, I don't blame you for being frustrated. If your person lets you sleep with her some of the time, why not all of the time? You get into certain habits, and they become safe and familiar. She sleeps in the same bed every night, so why can't you?

Why do cats like to sleep in bed? Because it's comfortable, of course! Beds were made for sleeping. They're big and soft and are covered with plush things like pillows and blankets. With people in them, they are even better. People are warm and snuggly. When we were kittens, we slept cuddled up to Mom or in a big kitten heap. This kept us warm and safe. And many of us still crave that comfort when we sleep. We always want to sleep next to the ones we love.

Why won't your person let you in the bed some nights, Freddy dear? Have you been running across her body in the middle of the night? A fun, invigorating play session before bedtime will help you settle in. Do you wake her up early in the morning? A late-night snack will help you wait a little longer until breakfast time. (However, be warned, Freddy, that people make a distinction between the days they go to work—when they get up on time for your breakfast—and the days they stay home—when they think they have the right to serve you breakfast very late. I do not advise you to allow your person to get into this habit. Make sure she wakes up to serve your breakfast at the same time every day.)

Have you been wandering under and over the covers, pawing to get in and then pushing to get out? Do you sleep on your person's head or chest? This is all perfectly understandable! After all, you need to keep warm, but when you get too warm, you need to cool down. Moving to different spots in the bed is a great way to regulate your temperature. Maybe she doesn't understand this.

Sometimes people think they have to lie perfectly still when you are in bed with them, so they won't wake you up. The responsibility ultimately becomes more than they can bear—plus, lying still for several hours can get a bit uncomfortable for your people. You must reassure them that there is no such thing as a cat with insomnia. If we are wakened, we can fall back asleep again in seconds. Demonstrate this to your person the next time she rolls on her side and wakes you up. While your first instinct might be to stalk off the bed with an angry stare, stop and think about it. Then look at her with a face that says, "No problem! I'm not even awake," quickly snuggle right back in next to her and fall asleep instantly. Perhaps then she will feel better about your being in the bed.

You might also try to pick one spot on the bed and stick to it. My person lets me sleep anywhere on the bed I like, but I generally settle down on the lower corner because she rolls over too much, and eventually it begins to bother me. I know this is not the ideal spot (I also spend a good part of the night under the covers curled up against her side, which I much prefer), but it's better than being shut out entirely.

If you two just can't seem to get comfortable together in bed, your person should buy you a cat tree or a window perch for the bedroom. A tree or perch is better than those little cat beds that sit on the floor, because we cats really prefer a bed with a view. If she turns over a lot, or if you like to move around all night, you might as well just make yourself comfortable on the perch she's set out for you, and you'll all be much happier.

If, for some reason I cannot imagine, your person absolutely doesn't want you in the bedroom, it's important for her to be consistent. At least this way you can settle down somewhere else for the night and get used to it. You'll still need a cat tree or a window perch, set up someplace where the curtains are open so you can observe the nightlife in your neighborhood. We cats are nocturnal, and we like to see what the other creatures of the night are up to.

When People Have Kittens

Dear Tabby,

My people seem to have had a kitten with no hair. I knew something big was coming because a few months ago they bought a lot of new furniture and rearranged one of the rooms in the house. They let me sniff it all and jump on it and even sleep on it, so pretty soon I felt like all that new furniture was part of my usual territory.

Then they put a tape player in the room with the new furniture and started playing this really awful music that sounded like 1,000 mice being eaten all at once. I really can't understand how they could like this music, but they just kept playing it, a little louder each time, until I got used to it. Then one day a friend of theirs came over with a tiny hairless human kitten, and that kitten made the same sound--only even louder than 1,000 mice! So I knew then it was a human kitten crying sound. Wow!

Anyway, they played with me and petted me and even fed me treats while that little kitten was around, so I figured these human kittens may be loud, but good things happen when they're around.

Then, a few days ago, my people got all excited and ran out of the house in the middle of the night. My man came home the next day and brought me a soft, cuddly blanket to sniff and sit on. It smelled nice, like something sweet. The next day my woman came home, too, and she had a little kitten with her. It smelled just like the blanket my man had brought home.

I thought it might be nice to have that little kitten around, except now they have visitors in and out of the house all day, and they don't pay any attention to me. I'm lonely even though the house is full of people. I'm trying my best to be adorable, but everybody thinks the new kitten is more adorable. What can I do?

Your cute but neglected fan,
Ricky

DEAR RICKY,

People call their kittens "babies," and they do pay an awful lot of attention to them, especially at first. Remember how helpless you were when you were a little kit? Your mom had to do everything for you—even teach you how to poop! Human kittens are just as helpless, and humans have to spend a lot of time taking care of them. Plus, it takes their kitten-babies almost a year to be able to do all the things feline kittens can do in just a few weeks! So while you were off to your new family by the time you were three months old, those human babies will be with their parents for eighteen *years* or more.

It's always seemed funny to me that humans are so proud to have just one baby, while we have six or eight kittens every time we give birth. But they think it's a big deal, and all their friends, family, and neighbors come by to admire the little hairless thing. Just make sure you have a nice, quiet place where you can retreat and hide while all those guests are coming and going, sweetie, because the stress can really get to even the friendliest cat.

Trust me, while it seems like the kitten-baby is the only thing in their universe right now, soon enough your people will get tired of the crying and fussing and smell and mess, and they'll remember that you, dear Ricky, are a lot less demanding and a lot easier to take care of. They'll feel tired and frazzled and overwhelmed, and they'll sit down on the couch and say, "Where's Ricky to sit here with me and just purr quietly?" They'll *need* you, sweetie, to help them keep calm.

It's nice that they took some care to help you get used to the idea that a new family member was coming. This tells me that they love you a lot and just need a little time to get over the excitement of the new baby. Keep being adorable, and try to spend some quality time with them after the company has all gone home. Rub up against them, snuggle with them in bed, or sit quietly with them on the couch. They'll remember how much they love you, and soon they'll be setting aside special time to play with you each day so you don't feel left out.

When these kitten-babies grow up, they can be a lot of fun to play with. They tend to like silly games a lot more than the adult humans, and don't get bored as quickly. Just be careful, because human children are kind of awkward and don't know how to be gentle with cats. Your humans will have to teach the young kit how to play with you nicely and to leave you alone when you're on your cat tree or in your bed.

And meanwhile, let me tell you a tasty little secret about kitten-babies. They almost always have some delicious, milky stuff around their mouths. You can lick it off, and your people will think it's adorable and love you for helping to keep the baby clean.

Someone's Been Sleeping in My Bed

Dear Tabby,

My life has been turned upside down, and I simply do not know what to do! My woman and I have been living together very happily for six years now. We get along well, have great playtimes, and we sleep next to each other in bed. I keep her warm; she keeps me warm--what could be better?

But lately a man has been coming over to the house more and more often. First of all, I'm not used to the way a man sounds and smells. His voice is deep, his footsteps sound different, and his clothes never smell the way a woman's clothes smell. When he walks into a room, he startles me. And when he's in the house, my woman hardly even looks at me. What's worse, I'm getting less playtime and less cuddle time with her.

Now my woman says he's coming to live with us. And Tabby, he is going to sleep with his head on the pillow next to her, which is *my spot* on the bed!

I have made it clear that I do not want

this intruder in my territory. I am very cool
with him, and when he tries to pet me, I hiss.
My woman thinks I'm jealous of her man, but
she is so wrong (as if a cat could ever be
jealous of a *man!*). I'm just upset because I
know my life will never be the same. We cats
are creatures of habit, Tabby, and we don't
like change. What can I do to make this man
go away?

Riled by romance,
Romeo

DEAR ROMEO,

If your woman really wants this man to move in, I'm afraid there's not much you can do about it. But I sympathize, O Romeo, because when a man moves in, he turns the house upside down. He brings in exercise machines and stereo equipment and shoes that smell funny. They move the furniture around, they buy new bookcases—the house is just a mess. Your routine is disrupted, your woman starts acting like this man is the center of the universe, and poor Romeo is left cowering in the closet and wondering when someone will remember to play with him.

The key to making the best of this situation, sweetie, is to turn things to your advantage. Remember, there will soon be two people in the house to serve you, instead of one. Teach the new man what you want—you can't stop him from moving in, so you might as well take advantage of him. He loves your woman and is going to want to do things that please her. Ingratiating himself with you will make him seem sensitive and sweet to her.

During this difficult transition, I recommend sticking to your routine as much as possible. Insist on being fed at your regular mealtimes, and meow, whine, and kick up a real fuss if your woman upsets your schedule. If she and her man come home very late, wait at the door with a few choice words to remind her that it's way past suppertime. You will feel more secure with a regular routine, and this may also encourage the man to feed you. It's a good first step—teaching him to feed you will get him started on caring for you in other ways. Plus, once he starts feeding you, you may find that you like him a little better. Reward him for his efforts by not hissing when he comes near you. Remember, positive reinforcement encourages good behavior.

You should also stick to your regular playtimes. If your woman is too busy mooning over her man, drag your toys out, sit in front of her, and make her feel guilty. Make your face say, "I can't believe you don't love me anymore." If her man picks up your toy and starts to play, encourage him. Sweet Romeo, I know you prefer playing with your woman, but, as I said, having two people in the house presents many positive possibilities. Take advantage of them! Men actually enjoy playing with cats; they admire our athletic ability and hunting skills. Play, using an interactive toy with a wand or a string, will help you both grow closer in a manly sort of way.

Of course, set your own pace when it comes to petting. Don't let him do anything that makes you nervous or uncomfortable. You may need to walk away or take a few moments under the bed to collect yourself when he tries to pet you. But try to keep an open mind, Romeo. If the guy feeds you and plays with you, how bad can he be?

As for sharing the bed, I'm afraid there's not much you can do about that. When he moves in, it's likely he and the woman will insist on it. But there's room in the bed for you, too. (Only the most heartless woman would kick her cat out of the bed for a mere man, and your woman sounds pretty nice.)

I haven't yet met a cat who can train a man to sleep across the foot of the bed, so you may have to surrender the pillow next to your woman. However, it's not difficult to teach a man to sleep on the diagonal or in an S shape to accommodate your preferred positions. If he's sleeping in a way that leaves you in a chilly or uncomfortable spot on the bed, or if he rolls over and disturbs you, just wake him up. You can do this by walking across his bladder or tapping him lightly on the face. If you're up by his face, stare right down into his eyes when he opens them. If you're down by his bladder, snuggle in between his legs and rest your chin on his ankles. Most people become paralyzed by this feline position, and you will be able to sleep undisturbed.

It may take some time to train him to sleep in a way that is most comfortable for you, but remember that he is not yet familiar with feline sleeping etiquette and try to be patient. Simply continue waking him up whenever he disturbs you (remember, this is called negative reinforcement), and he will learn quickly.

And please, dear Romeo, no matter how much you are tempted, do *not* sleep on the man's face. Your woman will not appreciate this, and you want to keep some peace in the family. Just give the guy a chance, and over time you may find yourself starting to like him.

Not Another Cat!

Dear Tabby,

I live a great life with my people. I eat good food, get plenty of toys to play with, and have a tall, strong scratching post. My litter box is always clean, and I sleep between my people on the bed at night. Sure, I miss them when they're gone all day, but they always come home. And we have great play sessions together where I make them both laugh. All in all, life is good.

But now they're talking about getting another cat. As if one cat--me, a gorgeous black cat with a long, silky coat--were not enough for them. How insulting!

I just know this will be a disaster. Another cat in *my* territory, using *my* things, eating *my* food! I don't know how I will be able to bear it. Do they really expect me to get along with this new creature? Don't they love me anymore?

Deeply disturbed and depressed,

Diva

DEAR DIVA,

Calm down, sweetie, because there are advantages and disadvantages to being in a two-cat family. Yes, there will be some competition for the attention of your people. Most likely you will have to share your toys, your cat tree, and even your spot on the bed. I know sharing territory is not easy for any cat. But I promise you will not have to compete with the newcomer for food—your people will put down extra food for the other cat. Trust me that this is true.

And think of how much fun it will be to have a fellow feline in the house who speaks your language. You won't have to struggle to make yourself understood with another cat: Every flick of your ears and change of posture will be clear. Plus, if your people carefully watch you two communicating and conversing, they can learn a little something about your language and may even come to understand you both a lot better.

And Diva, you will no longer be stuck with playmates who are awake all day and want to sleep all night. Your cat pal will be gloriously nocturnal, just like you, so the two of you can scamper off to the living room in the middle of the night and play jungle cats together. Sure, playing with the people is a lot of fun, but when they're asleep or not around, playing with another cat can be fun too.

You two may not ever get friendly enough to sleep to-gether, but if you do, it's a lot warmer to sleep curled up with a fellow cat than it is to simply curl up alone and cover your nose with your tail. Personally, I find the biggest advantage to be in the grooming department. Another cat may well agree to clean your ears for you—one area it is almost impossible for us to clean properly on our own. Remember, though, you must reciprocate—this is only fair.

Of course, dear Diva, we are not really like lions, who live in close family groups. But we're not really like tigers either, who prefer to live far apart and only hook up during the mating season. In fact, housecats who have gone wild (a concept I still have a difficult time accepting) usually live in packs where they have rather loose but very real relationships.

There are two secrets to successful feline introductions, Diva dear. The first is to do it gradually, just one sense at a time. The second is to make sure no cat is forced to share things she does not want to share. When your people bring the new cat home, even before you see him, he must be placed in a separate room with his own food, water, litter box, snuggly place to sleep, toys, and even a scratching post (we don't want him to get off to a bad start by scratching up the pullout sofa in the guest room, do we?). This gives him a chance to get used to his new house without worrying about annoy-ing you, and gives you a chance to get to know him without having to defend

your territory. Of course, your people should go in the room and play with him so he can start to feel safe and welcome. But make sure they also play with you to help keep your stress level low. After all, they have brought a new cat into *your* territory, and there's no denying the stress of that situation!

Remember, one sense at a time. So first you can talk to one another through the door. People get to know each other entirely by talking, with no sniffing involved (amazing but true!), but for us, sniffing is the more meaningful introduction. So after talking for a day or two, you can swap scents by each sleeping on a little towel and then having your people simply switch towels. After that, try switching rooms: You spend an hour in the new cat's room, and the new cat spends an hour exploring the rest of your house—all with the door closed between you. I don't have to tell you, Diva my dear, how much you can learn by sniffing the scents left behind by another cat, so this scent swapping is a crucial step.

Next comes a quick look. Simply have your people open the new cat's door, perhaps when you are at the far end of the hallway, so you can see the newcomer from a distance with no encroachment upon your personal space. If you both feel comfortable with this, they can open the door when you are a bit closer to the new cat's room. A little food bribe at a time like this wouldn't hurt, so you both are more focused on the food than on each other and so you realize there is no competition for food. Gradually, as things go well, they can leave the door open for longer and longer periods of time.

Of course, at first there is going to be some sniffing of derrieres, some posing and posturing (which, I will bet, Miss Diva, you can perform with the best of them). But if you keep the introductions slow and positive, with toys and play to distract you both if things get a little heated, you should eventually end up with a peaceful household. We cats are slow to make friends, especially with other felines (and there's nothing wrong with being particular about who you associate with; cats with discriminating taste are always dignified), but most of us do finally accept another cat.

Now, as for that second secret, even after the new cat comes out of his separate room, you two should always be fed from your own dishes, and they should not be placed so close together that you must bump into each other to eat. Mealtimes are sacred to cats, and we prefer to experience them in private. Two litter boxes are also a must: You may simply prefer that he not soil yours, and you have every right to make that demand. By now, the new cat will have covered his scratching post in his scent, so there's no harm in letting him keep his little totem pole and feeling that at least one thing in the house is his. And if you both like the same toys but want to play separately, you shouldn't be forced to share.

I definitely approve of a house with two feather sticks, two furry mice, two crinkly balls, and even more!

If you two get off on the right paw and feel comfortable with the way the intoductions were handled, Miss Diva, you may find you actually like having this new puss around.

I Think I'm Psychic

Dear Tabby,

I think I'm psychic. I always seem to know when my person, Craig, is sick or sad. Of course, you'll say, he takes out the extra box of tissues, he stays home from work, and drinks chicken soup. How could I not miss such obvious signs? But even when he doesn't do anything different, I can still tell.

Once Craig was really sick, but all he did differently was go to bed a bit early. Still, I knew he was in trouble, and I spent the whole night wrapped around his feet to keep him warm. And when he's sad, he doesn't cry or anything, but I still know. So I let him talk to me, and I don't give him any advice or tell him he did anything wrong. I just follow him around the house and push my head into his hand, so he knows I love him.

Tabby, I don't know how I can tell these things, but I'm always right. Do you think I have ESP?

Your (mind-reading) friend,
Bastet

DEAR BASTET,

While you are named after an Egyptian goddess, there is nothing supernatural about your powers to discern Craig's health and moods. It's not mind reading, it's body reading.

We cats have a wide range of words and sounds we use, but for us sounds are a minor way of communicating. Smells are major (as I pointed out in Part Three), but so is body language.

We talk with our bodies all the time. When our tails are up, for example, it means we're feeling great. When they're down between our legs, we're scared. When they're swishing from side to side, we're getting angry. The way we hold our ears, how we crouch, how wide we open our eyes, the position of our whiskers, even the way we settle (or don't settle) our hair all send messages that our fellow felines can read loud and clear.

We are masters at reading little gestures, body postures, and facial expressions. We know just from looking at them when other cats are mad, scared, happy, hungry, ready to fight, ready to mate, or ready to play. So we don't need anything so obvious as a giant pot of chicken soup to know when our people are sick. We can see it in their eyes, in the way they hold their shoulders, in the breathy "OY" sound they make getting up from the couch. We notice the little things they do that they are not even aware of. They may be able to hide things from their mothers, but, Bastet my dear, they can't hide anything from us.

So how do we use this special talent? Of course, we use it to be nice to our people. When they're sick, we snuggle up and keep them warm. When they're sad, we sit quietly and listen. We pay more attention to them and do the best we can to make them feel better and nurse them back to health.

Studies done by human scientists have shown that people who have cats recover more quickly from illnesses, get over stress more easily, and live longer than people with no cats. And this, my dear little feline goddess, is just one of the things that make us truly special. We have transformed a remarkable instinct to communicate into an even more remarkable instinct to heal.

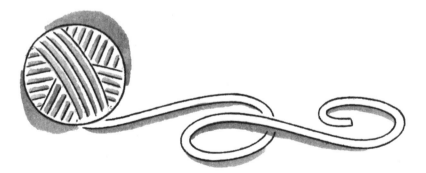

Tired of Talking to Myself

Dear Tabby,

I love to talk, but my people don't speak
my language. Sure, we can exchange some body
language--when I blink at them to show them
I'm feeling safe and relaxed, they usually
blink back, and I always flick my tail when
they say my name so they know I'm listening--
but I long for a deeper level of conversation.
Sometimes I try to teach them a few words of
feline, but they don't get it. They think I'm
just jabbering. I talk and occasionally I
sing, but I do *not* jabber! Have you ever heard
of people who can speak our language?

Longing to be a linguist,

Allegro

DEAR ALLEGRO,

Some human scientist with nothing better to do counted up all the sounds we cats use and decided we have a vocabulary of about 100 sounds. (Just for comparison—now I'm not picking on anyone here—dogs make about 10 different sounds.) Of course, humans make thousands of sounds, so while most of us understand their language, we never will be able to speak it with great fluency.

However, there are a few human words we can say, and I encourage all cats to learn them. They include *now* (which you can say when it's time for a meal), *yum* (for after the meal, to show your approval), *wow* (when they bring home an especially nice cat toy), *uh-oh* (for when you accidentally knock over the Tiffany lamp), and *mom* (I promise if you use this word to address your female person, she will do anything you ask). Learning these human words will help open up the lines of communication between you and your people.

I also think it's important to have specific names for each of your people so they know when you are speaking to them. Don't worry about what they call each other; just choose names that are easy for you to say. It's not important that they learn to say their own names—only that they recognize them and respond. Whenever you want to address that person, just look him or her directly in the face and say his or her name. Repeat, repeat, repeat—patience and persistence are the keys here. Eventually most humans do learn their names, and some even learn to come when we call them from another room.

Unfortunately, Allegro dear, just as we will never be able to speak fluent human, our people are unlikely to ever be fluent in feline. We communicate with a complex mix of sounds, postures, and smells that all work together to convey our message, and our people have very limited abilities to comprehend in all three ways at the same time.

However, I find it delightful to sing ducts with my person in the evening, and you may also enjoy this. Start by teaching your person to repeat just a word or two. It doesn't really matter what the words are—they can even be baby talk or nonsense syllables—because the pleasure here comes from the face-to-face attention and interaction. Pick a time when your person is quiet, then look her right in the face and say your word (a very easy word to start with, and one I taught my person in just a few minutes, is *meh*). Wait a moment, then repeat it. Keep repeating, but give her time in between each repetition to say the word back to you. When she finally does, reward her by rubbing against her leg, then looking up at her while your face says, "You are an extremely clever person, and I adore you." Repeat the sound again, just to

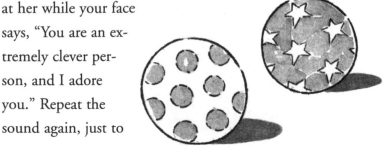

make sure she understands the game, and be sure to reward her for every correct answer.

Once you have taught your person the idea of repeating after you, you can begin to make up songs. Teach your person just a few phrases at a time—remember, it's not easy for them to speak cat—and don't forget to pause after each phrase so your person can repeat it. Eventually, you can sing to one another from different rooms of the house. This is a lovely way to keep in touch when you crave some interaction but don't feel like getting down from the windowsill or your people don't feel like getting out of bed.

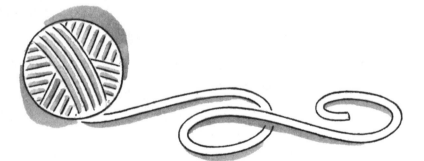

"Just Like a Dog" . . . ?!
How Rude!

Dear Tabby,

My person and I really like to do things together, and lately we have begun a special mission that I feel really proud of: We visit people who are living in hospitals or nursing homes. Those people are so happy to see a cat, and I sit on their beds and let them pet me and talk to me. I sometimes do little tricks for them, too, like jumping through a hoop or waving with my paw. I got ready for this important work by making lots of short little trips to other people's houses when I was a kitten and slowly built up to these visits, so it's never really been stressful for me. And now, my person is careful to make sure that when I start to feel tired or stressed during one of our visits, we go home.

It was actually fun learning how to do the tricks. I'm a smart kitty, and I like to do things that make me think. My person understands me, too, and has made it worth my while to learn this stuff by offering me treats and

lots of affection when I do my tricks. It's
pretty interesting sometimes to try to figure
out what she'd like me to do.

I really like these special visits. Everybody pets me and pays attention to me and
makes a big fuss. They're so happy when I
come, and I honestly think they feel better
when they're with me. And Tabby, what could be
more dignified than helping people feel good?

I think I'm a pretty typical cat, but the
other day I heard someone at the hospital say
I'm so smart and affectionate that I'm "just
like a dog." I'm so offended! They seem to be
saying that only dogs are smart and affectionate and love humans. I'm a cat, Tabby,
and I *don't* act like a dog! How could anyone
be so rude?

Intensely insulted,

Sweet Pea

DEAR SWEET PEA,

You, my poor little kitty therapist, have been the victim of dogism, a kind of species prejudice that sometimes rears its ugly muzzle among humans. Dogism means judging all animals as if canines were the pinnacle of pet evolution. Of course this is absurd, but the canine partisans have armies of lobbyists everywhere, spreading the dogist myths that cats are aloof or can't learn anything or don't really form attachments or don't care about their people.

Dogists see that dogs learn certain kinds of tasks very easily and think that means dogs are more intelligent. They see that dogs act more compliant (and even subservient) around their people and think that means dogs are more devoted.

These myths can be insulting but harmless, as when they encourage silly debates among humans on topics such as "Are dogs or cats smarter?" (As I'm sure you realize, little Sweet Pea, these types of questions are meaningless. Dogs are smarter when it comes to canine activities, and cats are smarter when it comes to all matters feline—of course!) But dogist myths can also foster a concept that has been devastating to thousands of cats every year: that housecats are really just wild animals who can simply be left in empty lots and will do just fine on their own. You and I know how much cats suffer in those situations.

For some reason, these dogist people fail to grasp the extremely simple fact that a cat is not a dog. You may be wondering, Sweetest Pea, how they could miss something so obvious. I think a little natural history lesson is in order. As I explained earlier to Morty, wild dogs live and hunt in packs. Their survival depends on their ability to cooperate and work together. A dog alone simply wouldn't live very long. In other words, dogs have brains that are wired to make them cooperative workers within a pack. They are desperate not to be alone, and will do *anything* (even behave in distinctly undignified ways) to avoid it. People often mistake this desperation for devotion.

In those dog packs, every dog has a place in the canine pyramid, from the top dog at the pinnacle on down to the lowly dogs at the base. All the dogs in a pack defer to the top dog—which is why obedience to authority is a natural part of being a dog. Nowadays, humans make up a dog's pack. They often mistake a dog's willingness to learn tasks that are useful to people as a sign of intelligence. But really, it's just an expression of the way dogs have evolved. For them, self-interest and pack interest are the same thing.

Cats, on the other hand, hunt alone (lions are the exception, of course). For wild cats, survival depends on their skills as individuals. That means even for us housecats, our brains are not wired for working cooperatively in groups. We don't need a pack to survive.

So we make different choices than dogs do. We are smart (supremely, incredibly smart), but we learn in different ways. We learn the things that interest us as individuals and that seem important to us. We're not designed to take orders from others (what a ridiculous idea!); we're designed to make sure we remain as comfortable as possible. Fortunately, because we are not always desperate for the company of a pack, we are infinitely more dignified as well.

What these dogists don't understand is that although we don't need to be among humans in order to survive, we *choose* to be among humans because we like them and we like our lives with them. We are seriously attached to our people and their world. We just view them differently than a dog does.

The dogists say all the good qualities of animals—loyalty, intelligence, ability to learn, affection, consideration—are canine qualities. But they're wrong. As you yourself have so eloquently demonstrated, Sweet Pea, a cat who is smart and easy to train and loving with people is not just like a dog—she's just like a cat!

Is It the Real Thing?

Dear Tabby,

I love my people, and they love me. Or at least, that's what I've always felt. But recently I heard some people say that cats don't really have emotions. They said we just cuddle up to our people so they'll feed us—that what seems like love is really just our survival instinct. Is this true?

Puzzled and perplexed,

Cleo

DEAR CLEO,

Absolutely not! If it *seems like* love, why does anyone think it isn't? How could any person live with a cat and not think we experience real emotions? I am as puzzled as you, my dear Cleo—and outraged as well. Denying a cat's emotions is the same as saying we are nothing more than our instincts. *Fleas* are nothing more than their instincts. Cats are the most complex creatures on earth.

There's no question that mealtimes are among the highlights of any cat's day, but so are playtimes, snuggle times, and purr times. How could every single friendly interaction we have with our people be about food? This is not even possible. Despite scurrilous rumors to the contrary, well-fed cats do not think about food every moment of their lives. When we are sweet to our people, we are not bribing them to keep feeding us. We are loving them.

Most ethologists (those are human scientists who study the behavior of animals) now agree that animals have thoughts and feelings. These ethologists act as if it were an exciting new discovery that we are not little machines who run around on automatic controls, eating and reproducing. But the people who live with us have always known that we experience joy and grief and fear and pleasure and comfort and love.

Anyway, why would anyone want to ask a scientist about these things? After all, how do humans know when they love someone? Certainly not by doing science experiments! They know by the way they treat each other, by the way they look at each other, by the way they are concerned for each other and always seek out each other's company. People who love one another never get bored with each other, always try to listen carefully, and take special care when someone is feeling bad. In short, people know someone loves them by the way they act. Cats do all those things, too. And that's how our people know we love them.

Why would people deny the experience of their own lives and hearts? Sometimes it's hard for humans to trust what they see and feel. But we cats know what's true. We have rich emotional and spiritual lives. Our people see it in the way we act. They see it in our faces. They see it in our eyes. In their hearts, they know it's the real thing.

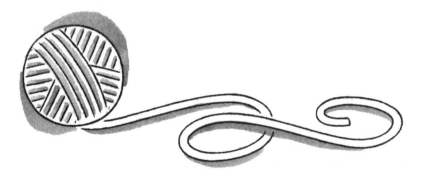

DEAR PEOPLE

While I wrote this book expressly for cats, it has always been my wish that some of you would decide to read it anyway. Now that you've come to the end, I hope you've gained some insights into the way we cats see the world.

If there's one thing I want you to remember from these letters, it's that we cats are not like you. We can learn from you, and you can learn from us, but our world is not your world. We can never deny our true nature or stop being what we are—animals.

And animals are not humans. We don't think the way you do; we don't experience the world the way you do. We have our own complex inner lives. We have feelings, but they're not always the same feelings you have. So, for example, we don't pee outside the litter box to get back at you for going on vacation or scratch the couch because we don't like your new beau. We don't have feelings of spite or jealousy. We are simply reacting to the world around us in typically feline ways. Please try to remember that the next time you see us doing something you think is naughty or undignified.

We do feel stress, though, and sometimes we try to tell you this with behaviors that you don't appreciate. Maybe we pee on the rug or hiss at you or scratch up the table leg or hide in the closet all day. A cat will tell you his limitations: "Enough petting," "This game is too rough," "I'm afraid," "I don't like that." You just need to pay attention. The next time you feel angry with one of my feline comrades, stop and think for a moment: "What is my cat trying to tell me? What's going on in her world?"

We also feel love, and we try to tell you that as well. We snuggle up close, we ask you to play with us, we rub up against you, we sleep on your head, we extend our noses to yours in dignified, heavenly nose kisses that we reserve for only our closest feline friends—and our favorite people.

You've reached the end of this book, so put it down and go offer a nose kiss to your cat right now. Get down to eye level with your cat, a foot or so away from her. Then slowly extend your face forward to her nose. If you've never nose kissed with your cat before, she may not immediately realize that this gesture of feline affection is coming from her person. Try gently sniffing as you move toward her, but don't get too close; let your cat come give you a kiss. Be still as your sweet cat extends her nose for a soft, gentle sniff.

Not all cats are nose kissers—although most are—but the more you love us, the more we love you. I promise, it's true!

Nose kisses to you and all the cats who live with you,
Tabby
>^..^<

ABOUT THE AUTHOR

Dear Tabby is the *nom de plume* of Yin Yin, a very wise and talented brown tabby cat with exceptional training and language skills. She lives in Brooklyn with two other cats and two well-trained people. One of these people is Beth Adelman, the editor of the on-line magazine *The Daily Cat*, the former editor of Cats magazine and *DogWorld*, and the managing editor of the *AKC Gazette*. Beth is also currently an editor for pet book publisher Howell Book House. She has won several awards from the Cat Writers Association and the Dog Writers Association of America, and is currently on the board of directors of the Dog Writers Educational Trust.